Why Dogs Are Better Than Kids

Why Dogs Are Better Than Kids

Jennifer Berman

**Andrews McMeel
Publishing**

Kansas City

Library of Congress Cataloging-in-Publication Data
Berman, Jennifer, 1961–
Why dogs are better than kids/Jennifer Berman.
p. cm.
ISBN 0-7407-0987-9 (pbk.)
1. Dogs—Caricatures and cartoons. 2. Children—Caricatures and cartoons. 3. Human-animal relationships—Caricatures and cartoons. 4. American wit and humor, Pictoral. I. Title.
NC1429.B38 A4 2000
636.7'002'07—dc21   00-030453

ATTENTION: SCHOOLS AND BUSINESSES

Andrews McMeel books are available at quantity discounts with bulk purchase for educational, business, or sales promotional use. For information, please write to: Special Sales Department, Andrews McMeel Publishing, 4520 Main Street, Kansas City, Missouri 64111.

FOR MATT, WHO'S EVEN **BETTER** THAN MOST DOGS

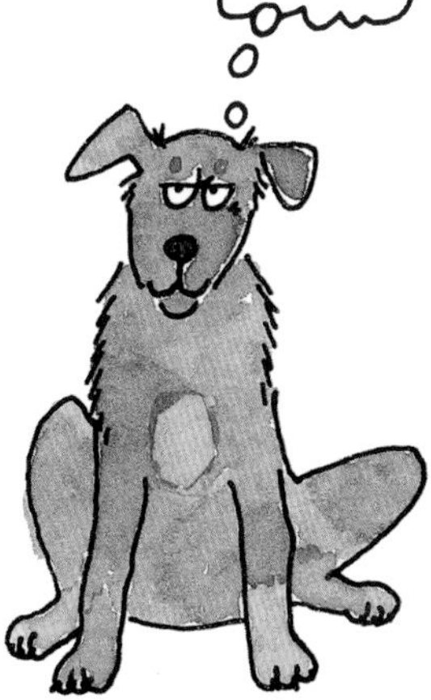

THANKS TO:

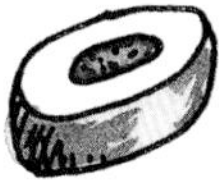

JO-LYNNE WORLEY and JOANIE SHOEMAKER, GREAT HUMAN BEINGS and GREAT AGENTS

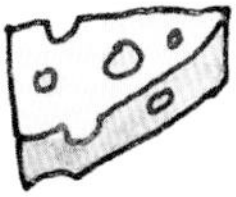

JULIE ROBERTS, FOR EXCEPTIONAL EDITORIAL WISDOM

SOY→ 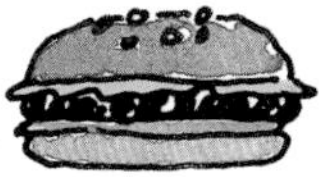

MY FAMILY, FOR EVERYTHING

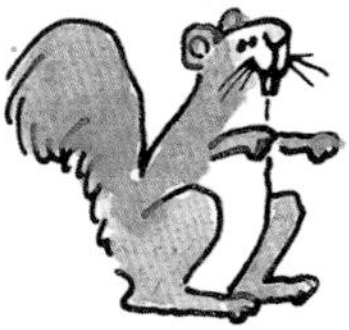

MY AMAZING FAMILY OF FRIENDS, ESPECIALLY THE YOUNG 'UNS, WHO, WITHOUT REMUNERATION OR SELF-CONSCIOUSNESS, MADE THIS LITTLE WORK POSSIBLE

PART 1:
WHY DOGS ARE BETTER THAN KIDS

YOU'RE NOT SORE FOR WEEKS AFTER YOU
GET A NEW PUPPY

IF YOUR DOG IS A FUSSY EATER, YOU CAN JUST LET IT GO WITHOUT FOOD UNTIL IT GETS GOOD AND HUNGRY

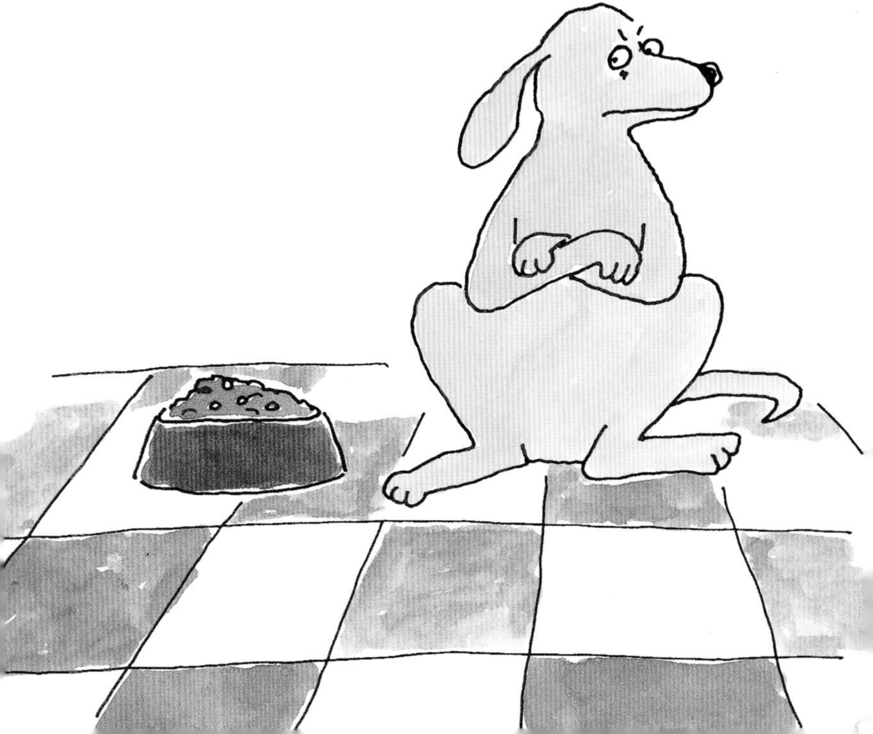

ADOPTING A DOG OF A DIFFERENT COLOR IS NO BIG DEAL

(AND IT DOESN'T COST $30,000.00 !!!)

AVERAGE COST OF SENDING A DOG TO SCHOOL - $42.00

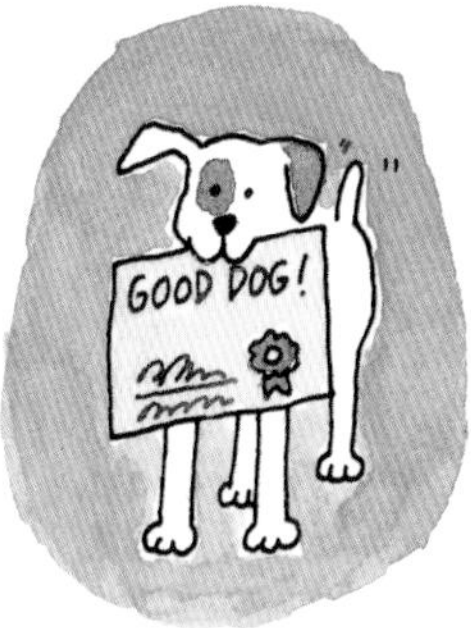
GOOD DOG!

AVERAGE COST OF SENDING YOUR KID: $103,000.00

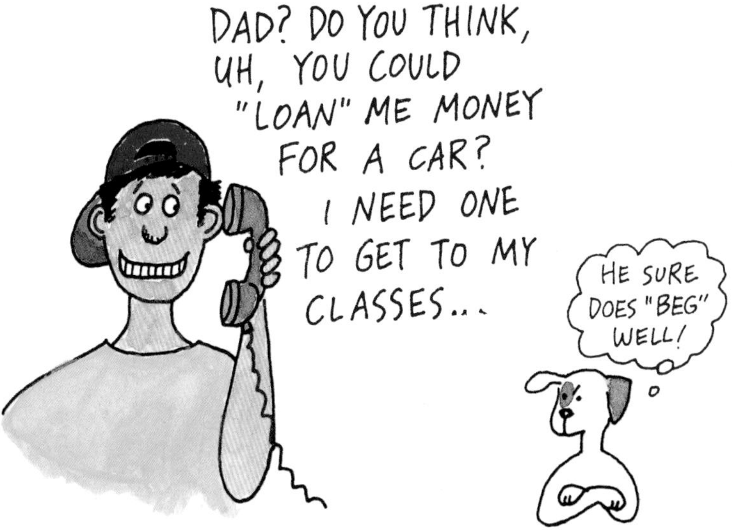
DAD? DO YOU THINK, UH, YOU COULD "LOAN" ME MONEY FOR A CAR? I NEED ONE TO GET TO MY CLASSES...
HE SURE DOES "BEG" WELL!

IF YOUR DOG IS REALLY, REALLY AWFUL, YOU CAN FIND A "FARM" TO TAKE IT

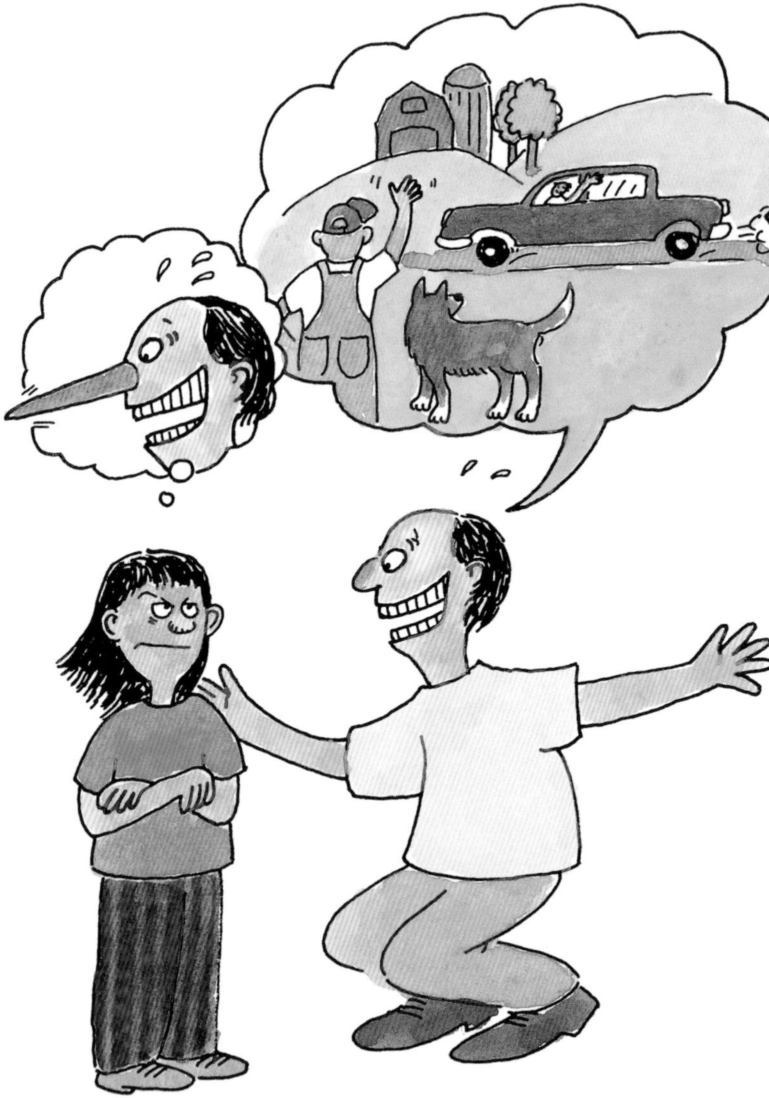

IT DOESN'T TAKE 45 MINUTES TO GET A DOG READY TO GO OUTSIDE IN THE WINTER...

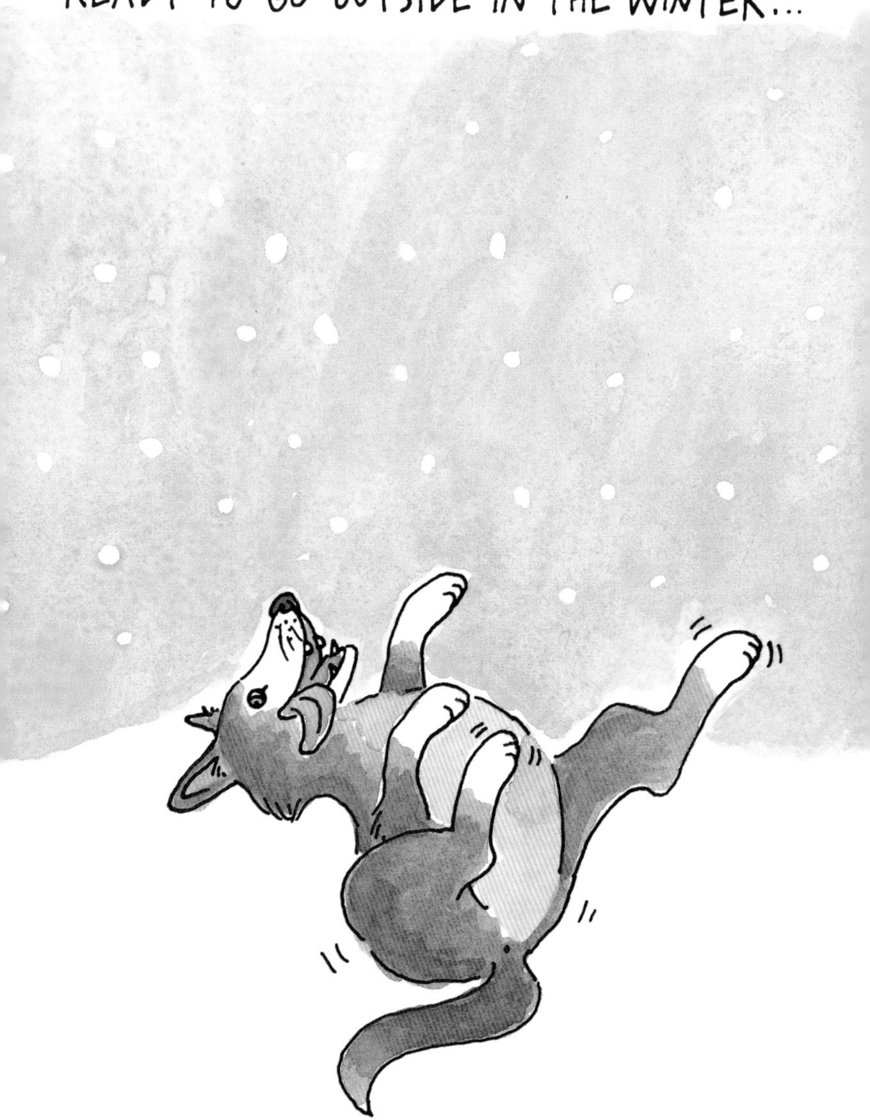

... AND IF HE HAS TO PEE, HE JUST DOES IT

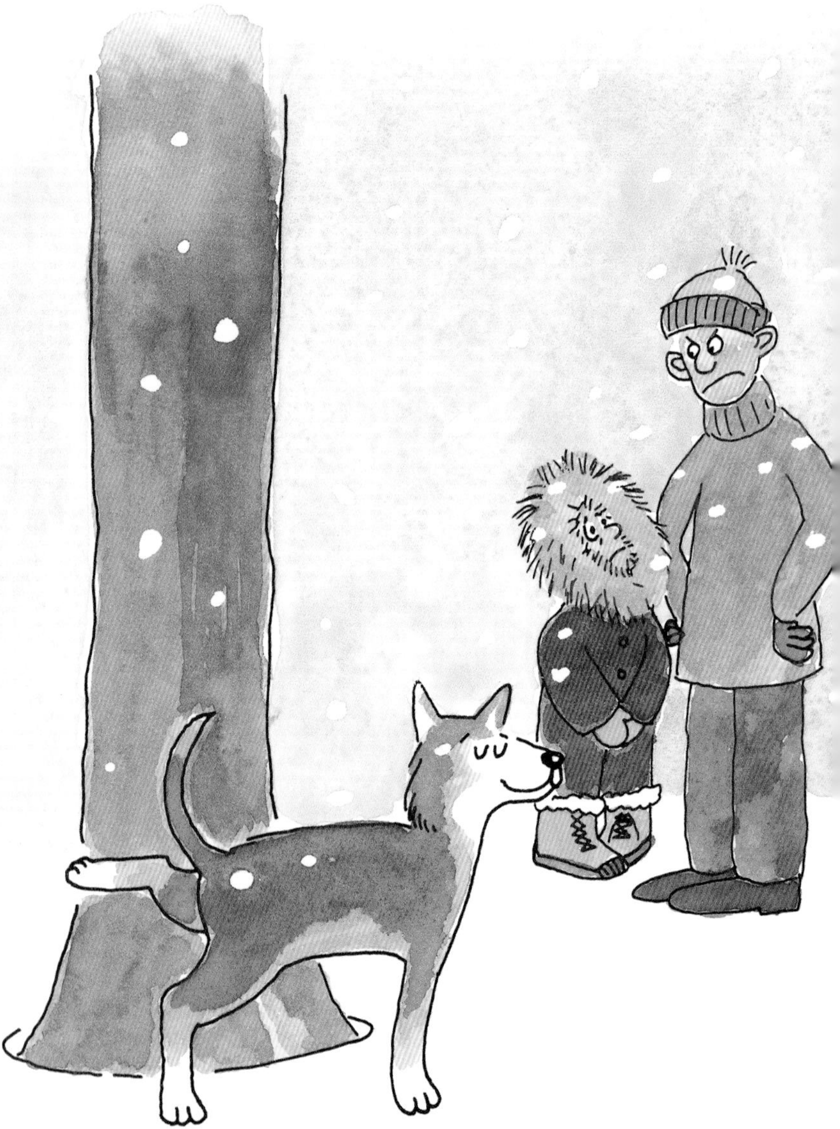

DOGS WILL NEVER ACCUSE YOU OF NOT BEING COOL ENOUGH

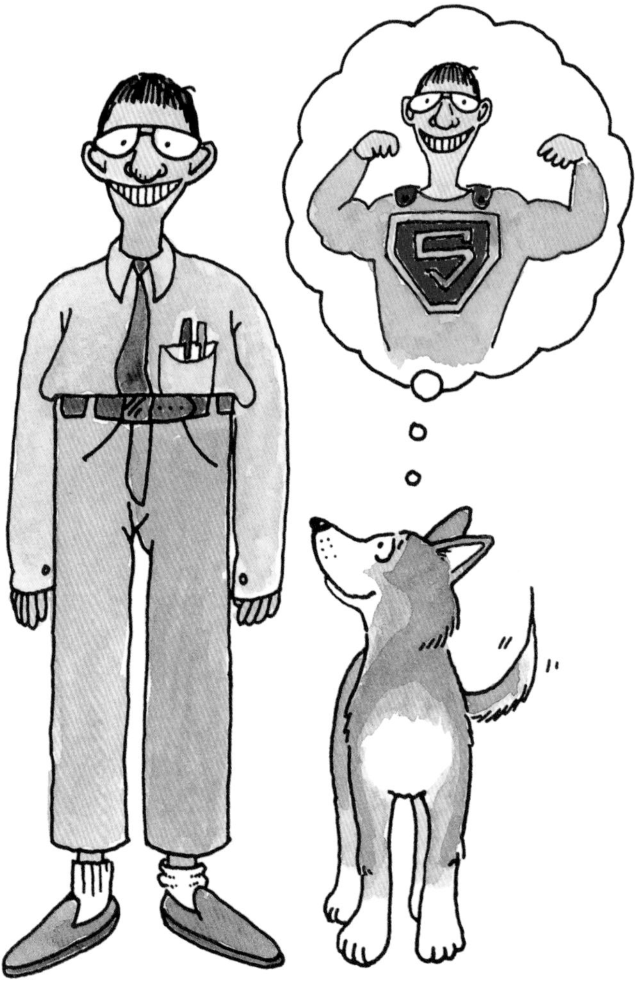

NO ONE WILL CRITICIZE YOU (OR YOUR DOG)
IF HE NEVER LEAVES HOME

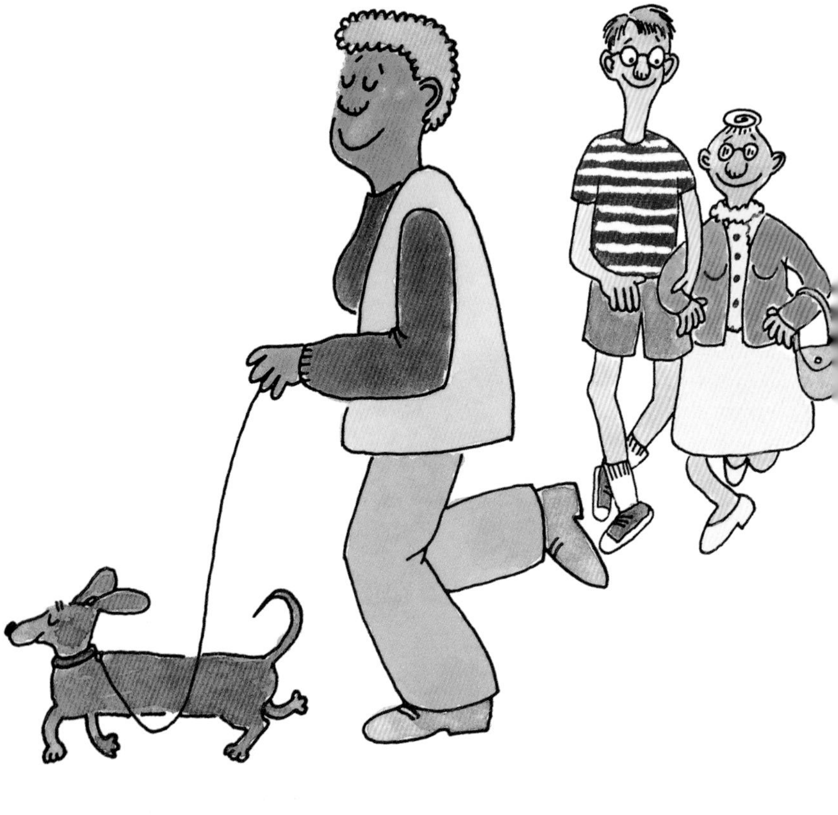

DOG GAMES DON'T REQUIRE ANY RAM *

* UNLESS YOU HAVE A BORDER COLLIE...

DOGS CLEAN THEIR OWN BUTTS

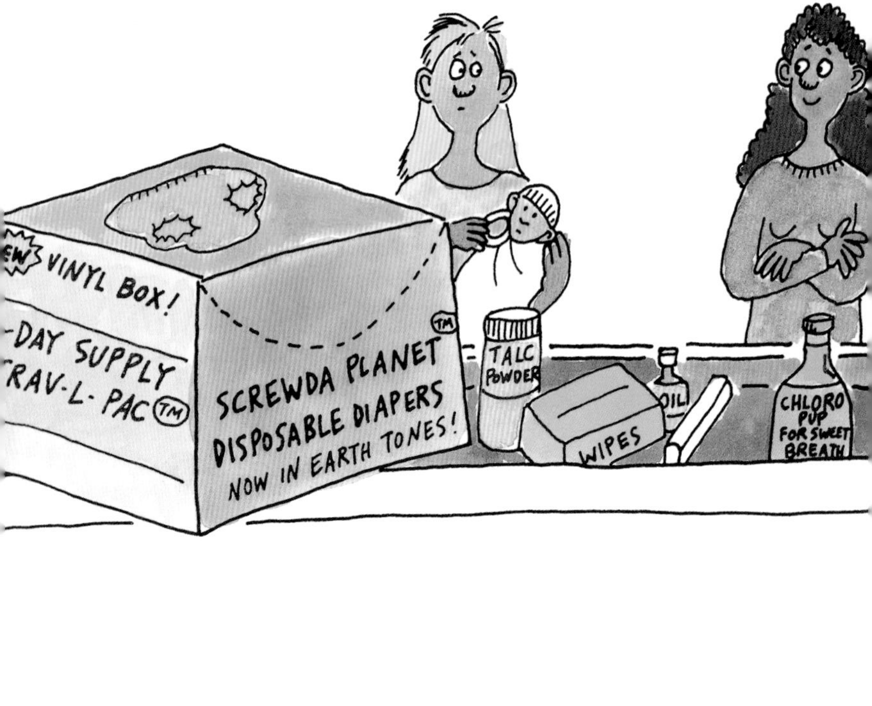
NEW VINYL BOX!
-DAY SUPPLY
TRAV-L-PAC TM
SCREWDA PLANET TM
DISPOSABLE DIAPERS
NOW IN EARTH TONES!
TALC POWDER
OIL
WIPES
CHLORO PUP
FOR SWEET BREATH

DOGS DON'T HAVE A DEATH WISH FOR THEIR SIBLINGS

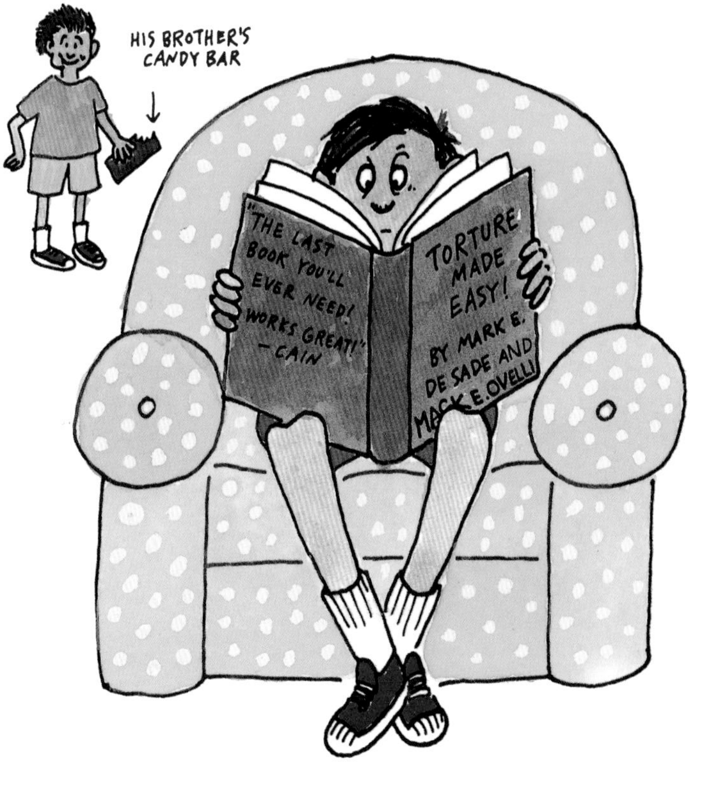
HIS BROTHER'S CANDY BAR
"THE LAST BOOK YOU'LL EVER NEED! WORKS GREAT!" — CAIN
TORTURE MADE EASY!
BY MARK E. DE SADE AND MACK E. OVELLI

DOGS APPRECIATE ALL THE TIME YOU PUT
INTO HOME-COOKING

AND THEY EAT MOST OF THE FOOD THEY FLING
ONTO THE FLOOR

DOGS CANNOT LIE

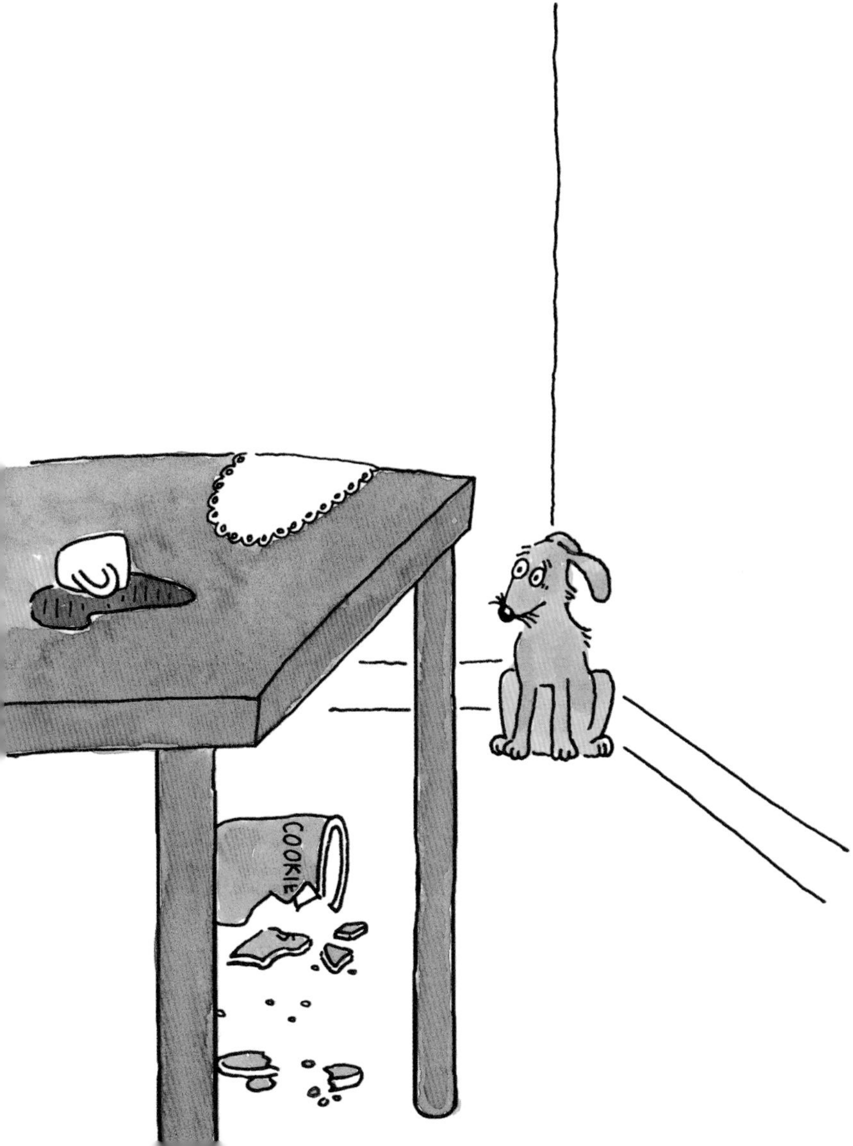
COOKIE

DOGS DON'T PULL LEGS OFF OF SPIDERS

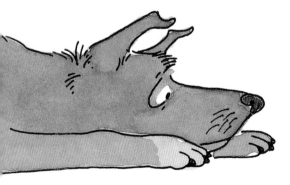

IF YOU MOVE, YOU DON'T HAVE TO WORRY ABOUT YOUR DOG MAKING NEW FRIENDS RIGHT AWAY

DOGS NEVER RESIST NAPTIME

DOGS DON'T INSIST UPON SINGING INSIPID SONGS OVER AND OVER AND OVER

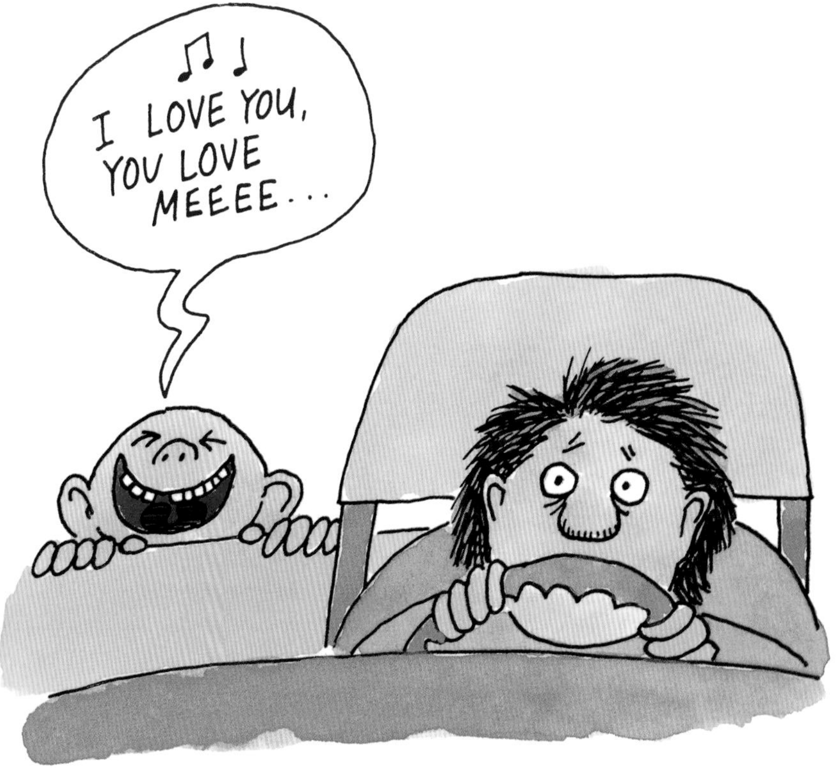
I LOVE YOU, YOU LOVE MEEEE...

DOGS DON'T INSIST UPON THE NEWEST COLLAR EVERY MONTH

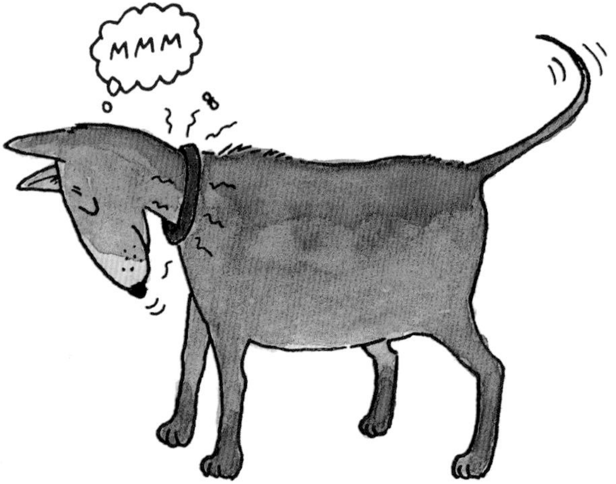
MMM

... BUT EVERY YEAR OR SO, THEY PROBABLY SHOULD BE "FRESHENED"

IT'S MORE ACCEPTABLE TO LOCK SCARY DOGS IN THE BASEMENT WHEN COMPANY COMES

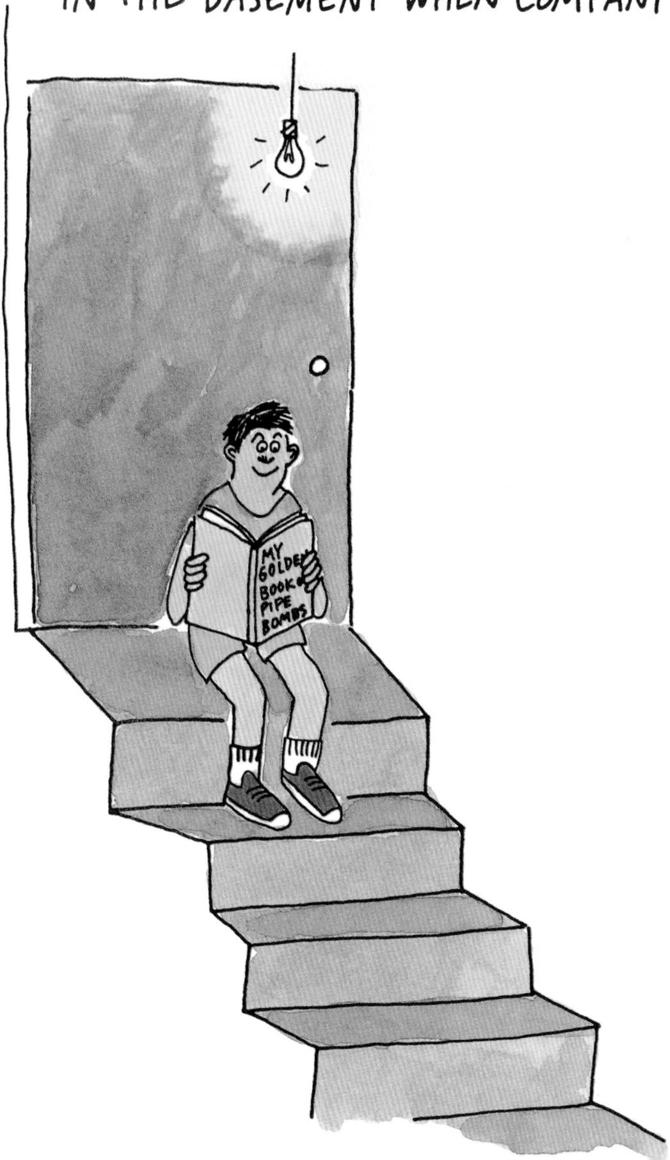
MY
GOLDE
BOOK
PIPE
BOMBS

DOGS DON'T REPEAT WHAT YOU'VE SAID ABOUT YOUR FRIENDS

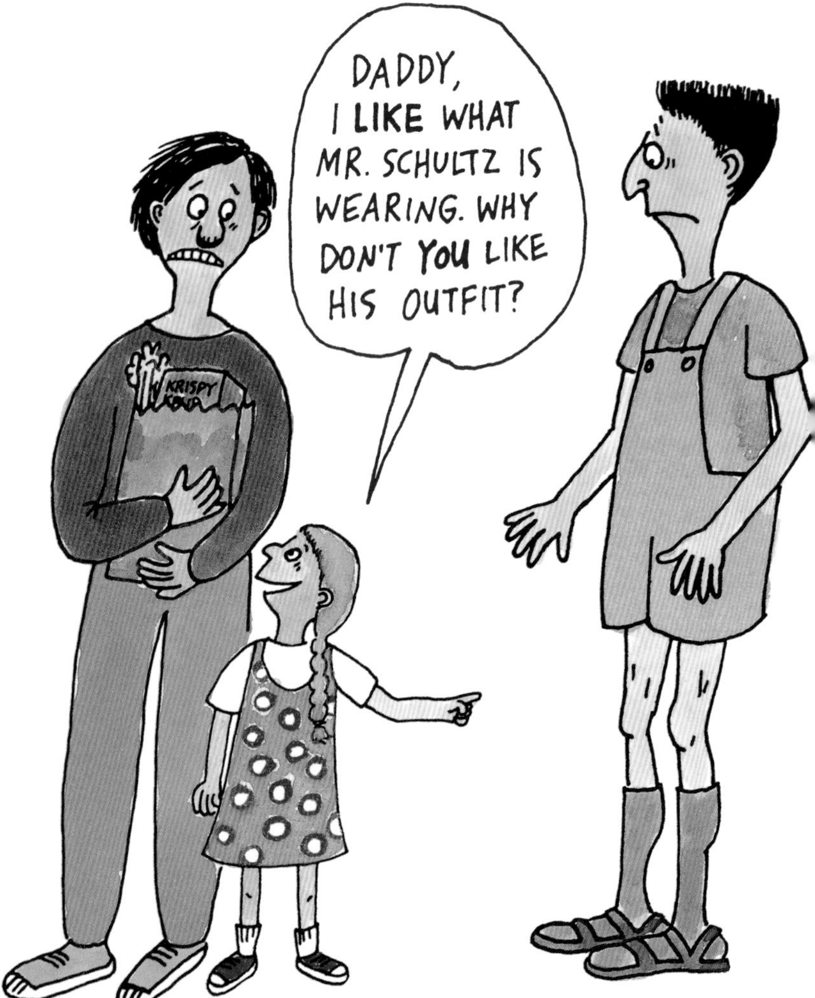
DADDY, I **LIKE** WHAT MR. SCHULTZ IS WEARING. WHY DON'T **YOU** LIKE HIS OUTFIT?
KRISPY

YOU LOOK **FORWARD** TO YOUR DOG'S TEENAGE YEARS

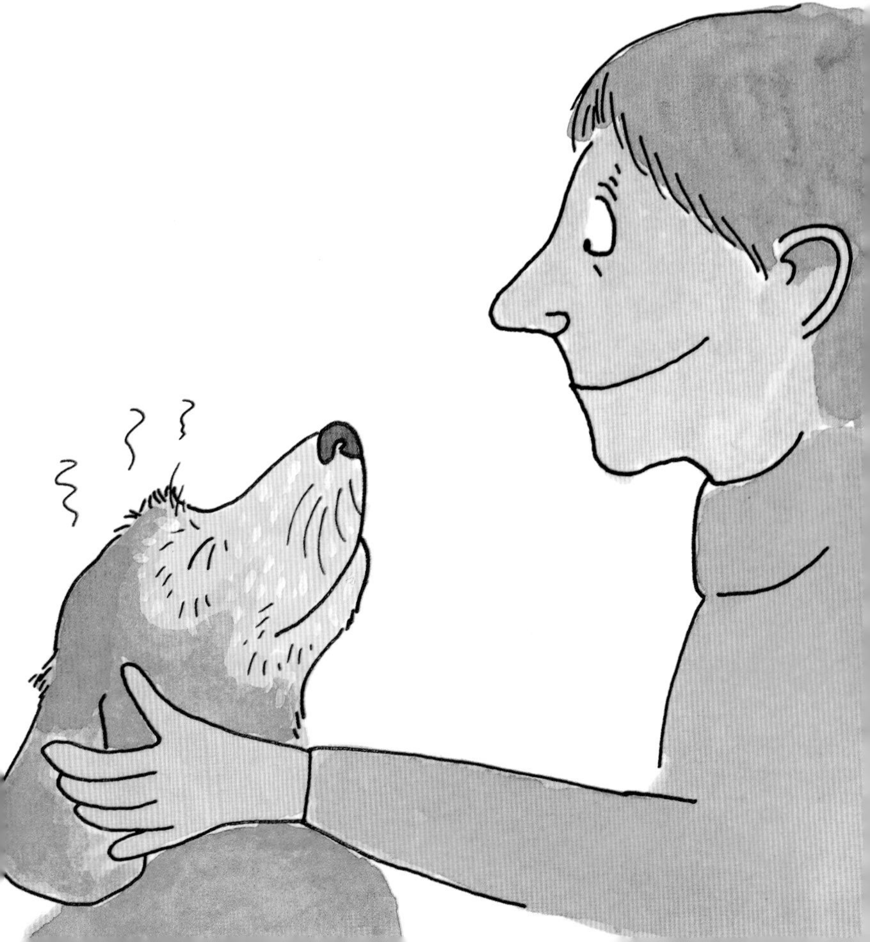

DOGS AREN'T INTERESTED IN ANY ANIMAL THAT ISN'T ANATOMICALLY COMPLETE

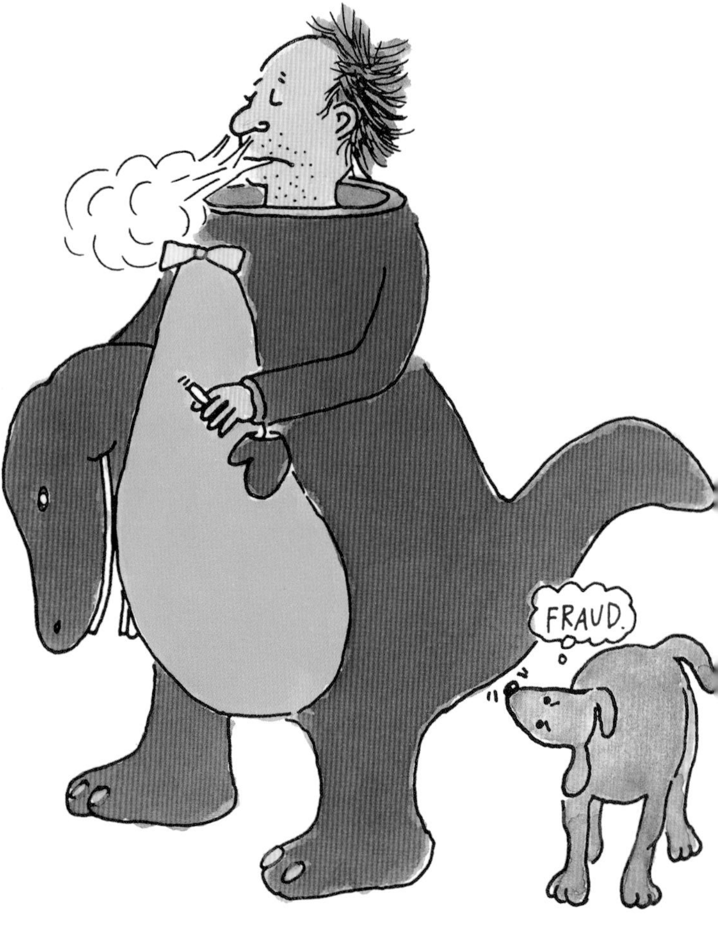
FRAUD.

YOU DON'T NEED EXTRA PHONE LINES FOR A DOG

BUT YOU MIGHT NEED SOME EXTRA **CORDS**

DOGS DON'T PESTER YOU ABOUT GETTING A KID

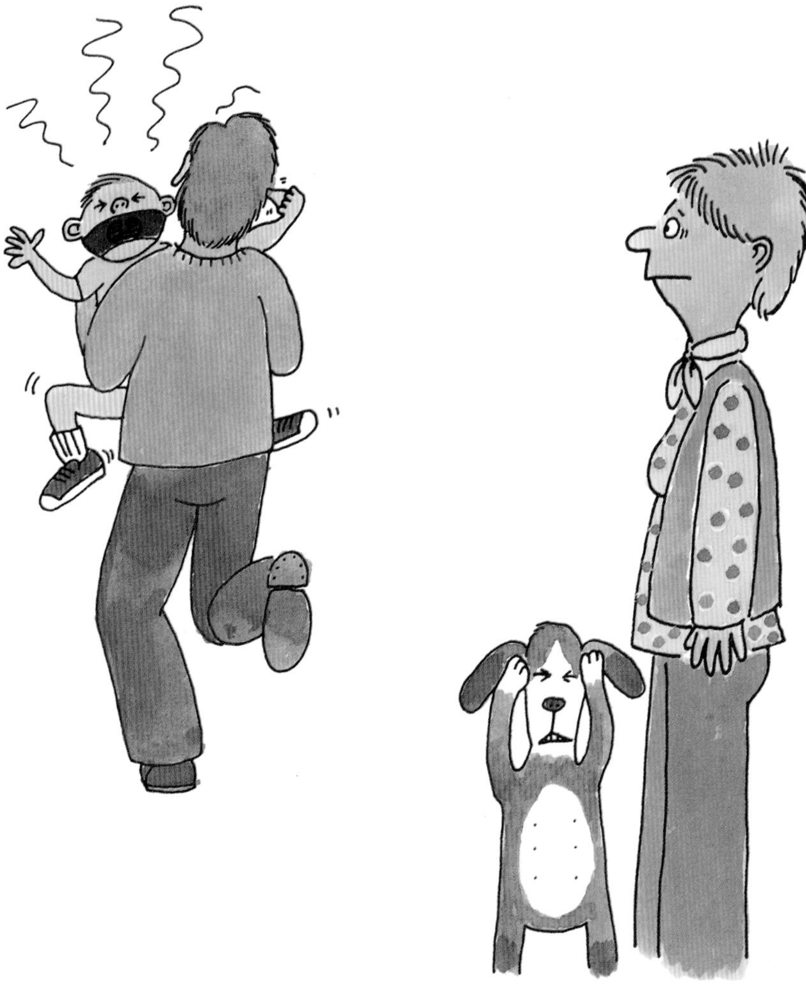

MALE PUPS ARE NOT OBSESSED WITH GUNS

RETRIEVABLE OBJECTS

SMALL, QUICK, MAMMALS

FOOD

MORE FOOD

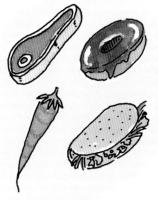

THE FOUR MAJOR DOG OBSESSION GROUPS

YOU DON'T HAVE TO WORRY ABOUT YOUR DOG REJECTING YOUR CHERISHED POLITICAL BELIEFS

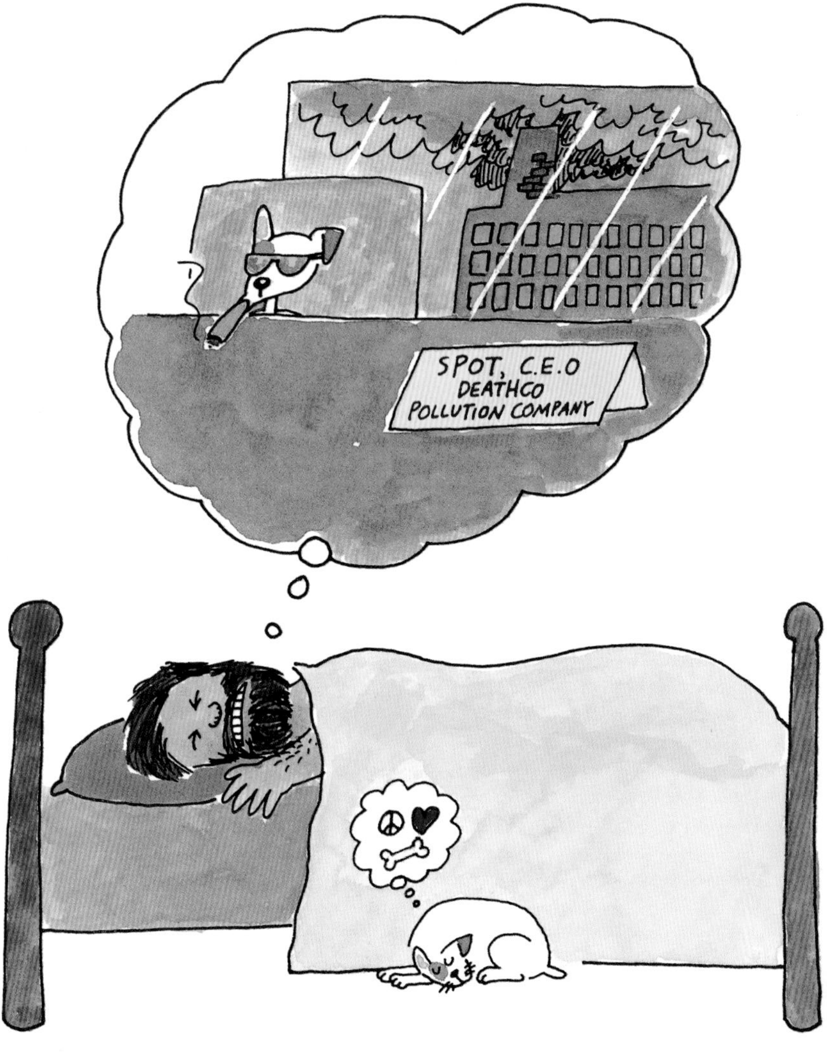

SPOT, C.E.O
DEATHCO
POLLUTION COMPANY

TEENAGE DOGS ACKNOWLEDGE YOUR VISITORS

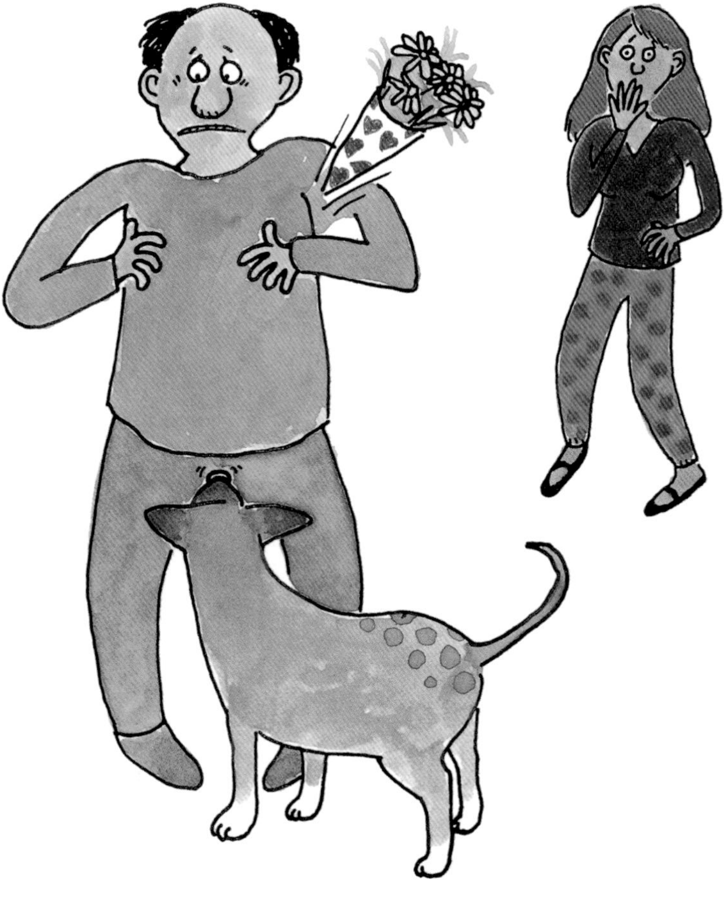

DOGS DON'T SPEND THEIR FIRST THREE MONTHS VOMITING ON YOUR SHOULDER

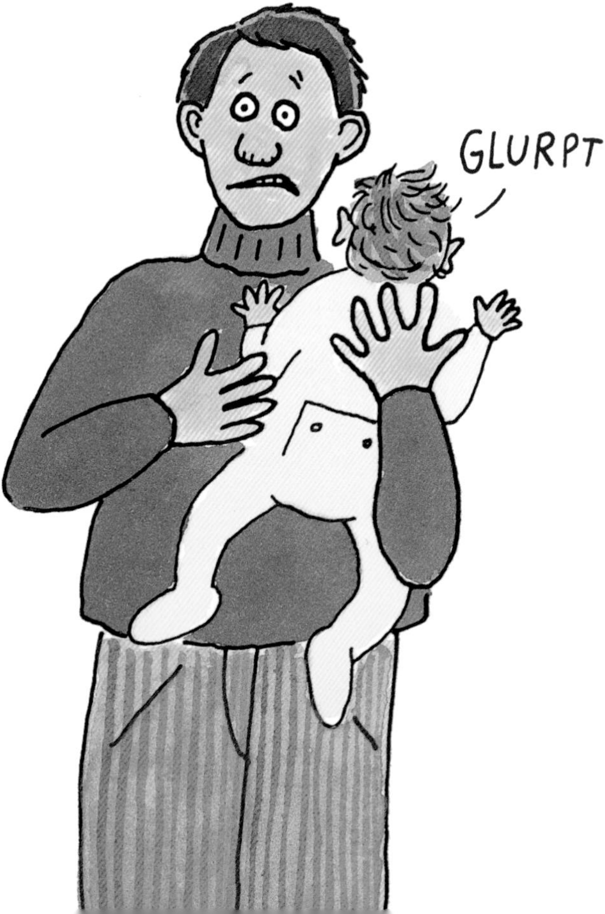
GLURPT

WHEN A **DOG** IS TWO, SHE'S **TWO**

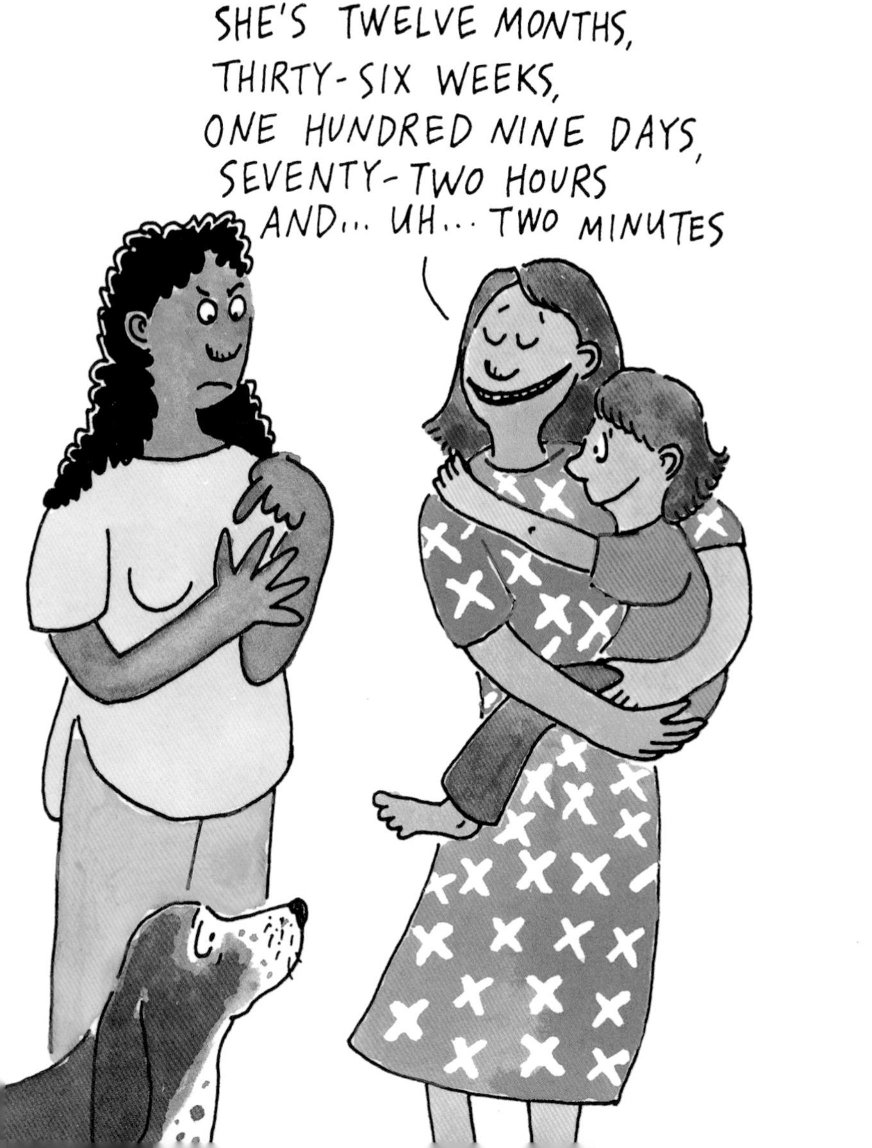

IT'S NOT CONSIDERED BAD FORM TO TIE YOUR DOG TO A POST WHEN YOU GO SHOPPING

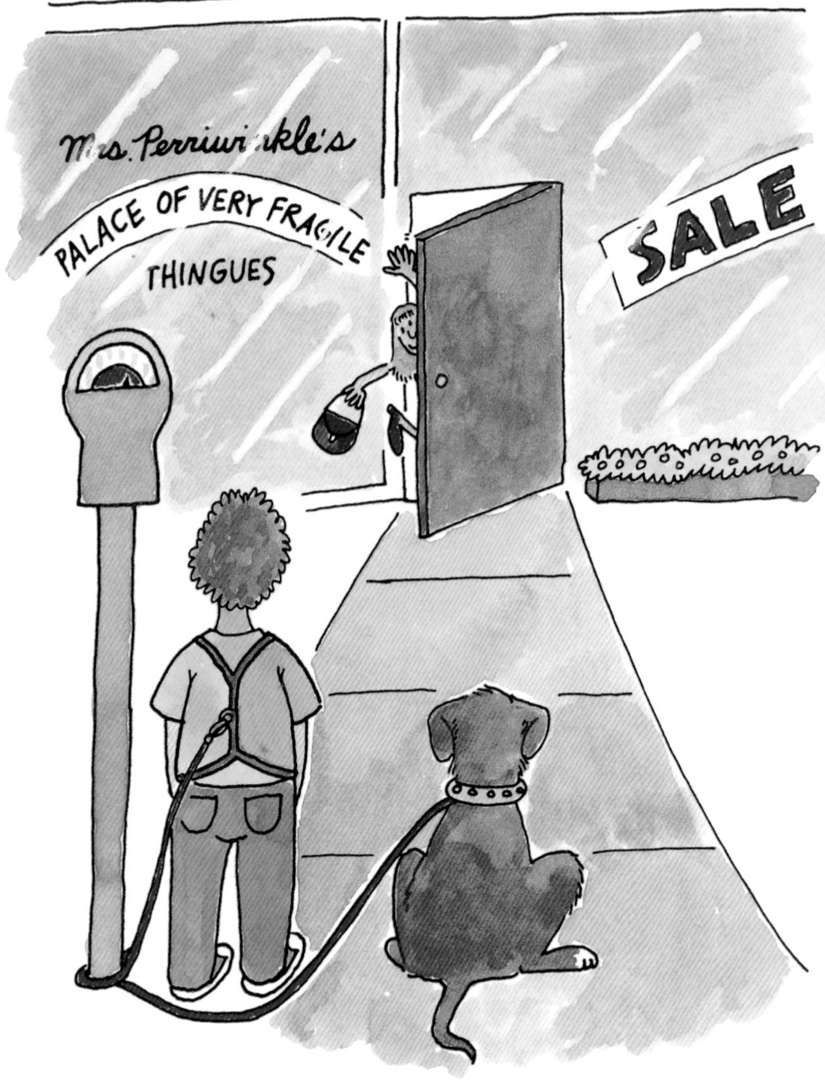
PALACE OF VERY FRAGILE
THINGUES
SALE

DOGS DON'T MIND MODEST BIRTHDAY FESTIVITIES

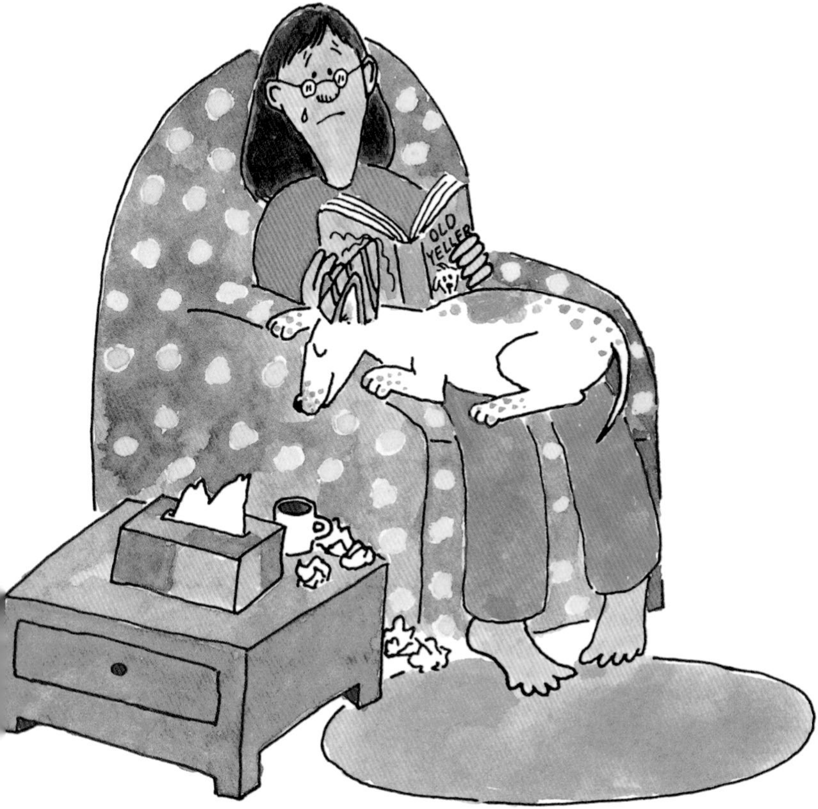
OLD YELLER

A DOG WILL NEVER WRITE A VICIOUS MEMOIR ABOUT YOU

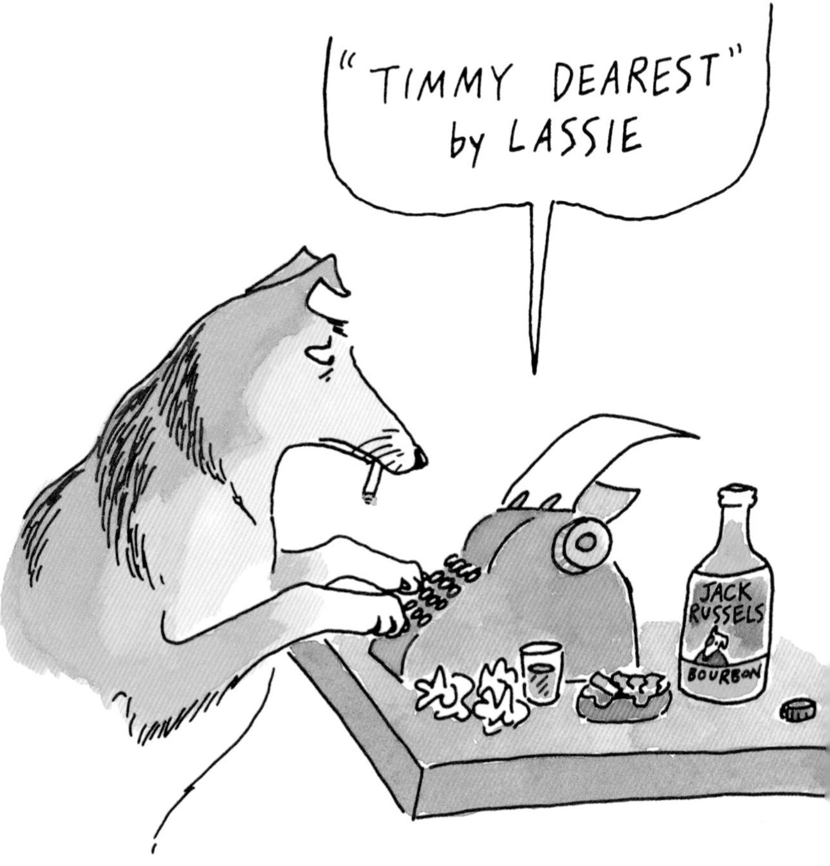
"TIMMY DEAREST"
by LASSIE
JACK RUSSELS
BOURBON

YOU CAN MAKE **SURE** YOUR DOG NEVER BECOMES A TEENAGE FATHER

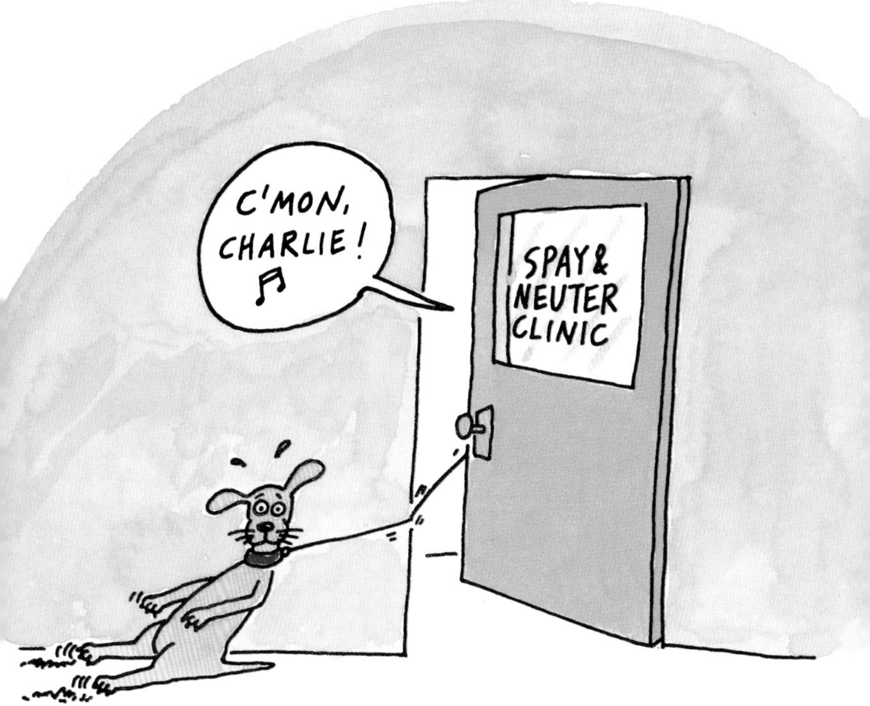
C'MON, CHARLIE! ♫
SPAY & NEUTER CLINIC

DOGS DON'T CARE IF THE PEAS HAVE
BEEN TOUCHED BY THE MASHED POTATOES

IF YOUR DOG IS A BAD SEED, YOUR GENES CANNOT BE BLAMED

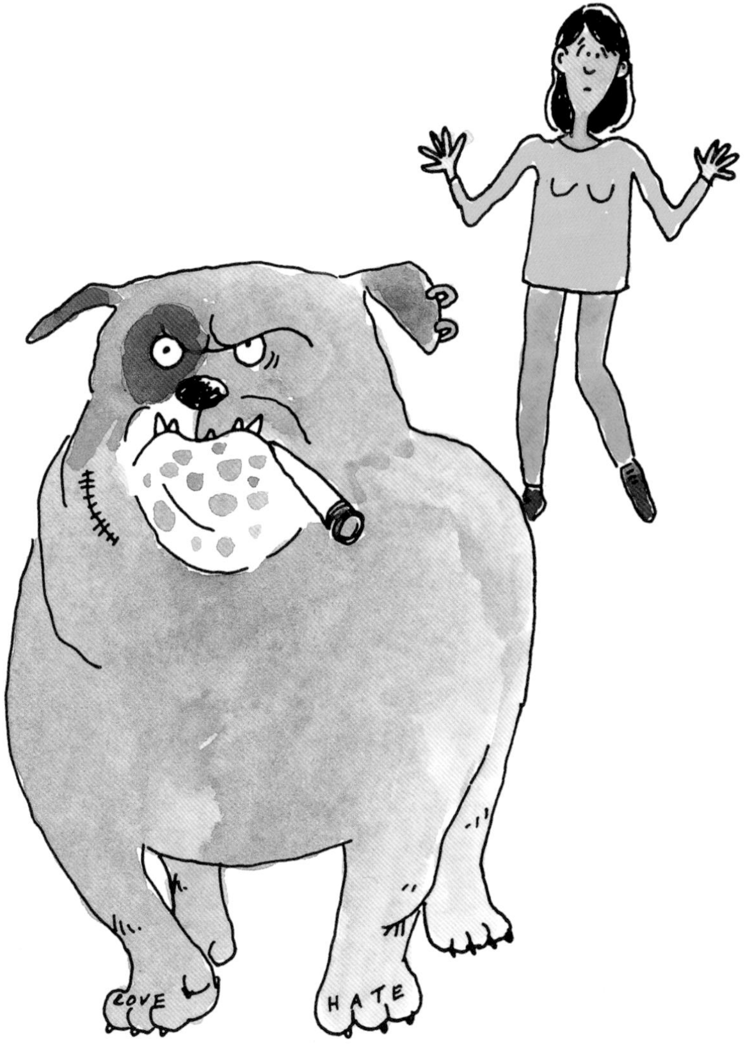
LOVE
HATE

DOGS NOTICE WHEN YOU COME HOME FROM WORK

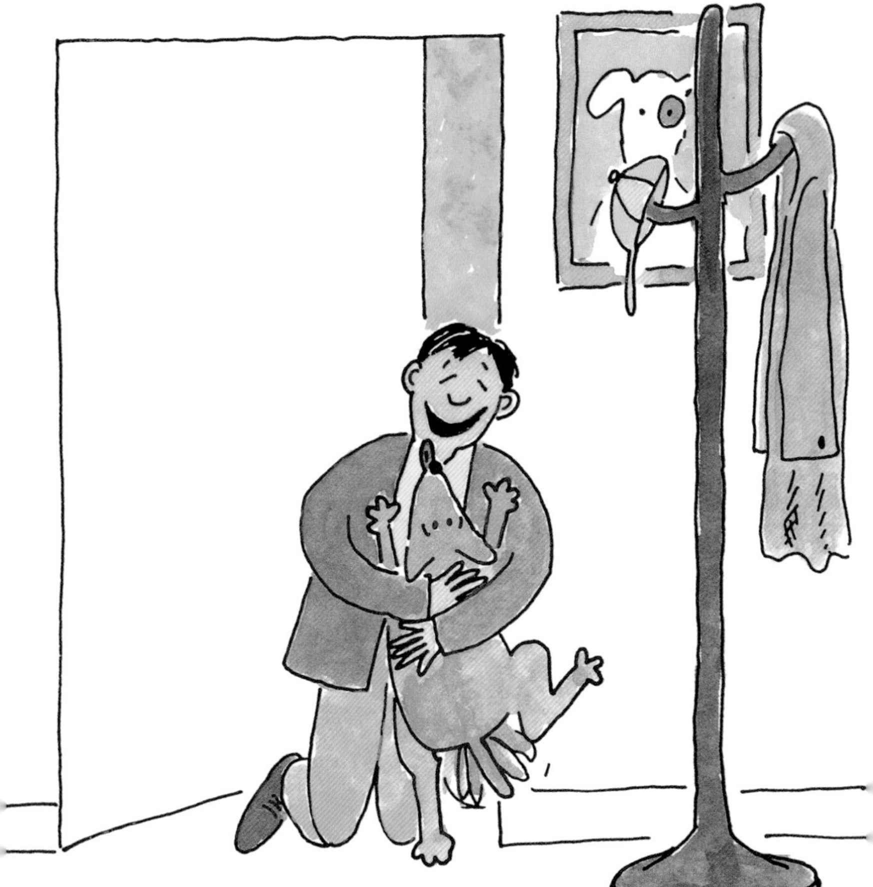

DOGS ARE HOUSEBROKEN BY THE TIME THEY ARE TWELVE WEEKS OLD

AND THEY NEVER CONTRIBUTE TO CHOKING UP LANDFILLS WITH DIAPERS

YOU CAN HAVE YOUR FIRST DOG WHENEVER YOU FEEL READY TO (AND YOU WON'T BE IN THE CENTER OF A MEDICAL ETHICS DEBATE)

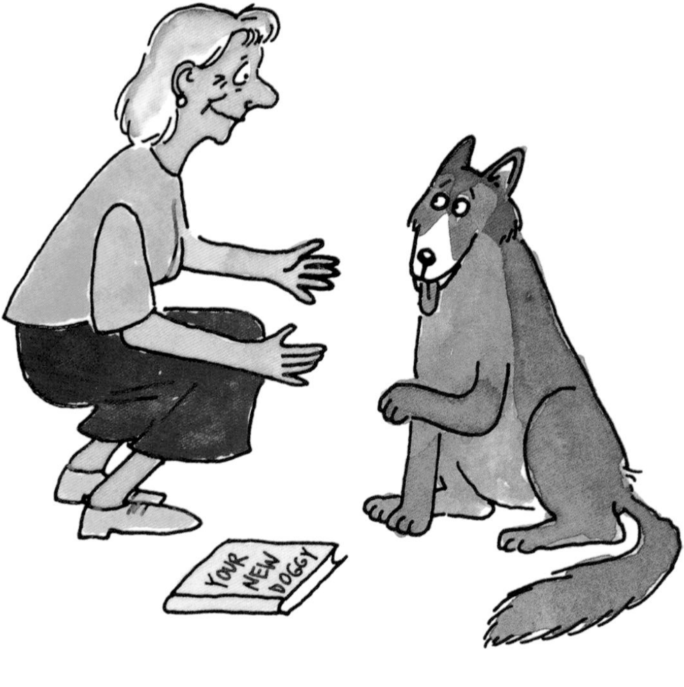
YOUR NEW DOGGY

TEENAGE DOGS ARE VERY EASY TO BE AROUND

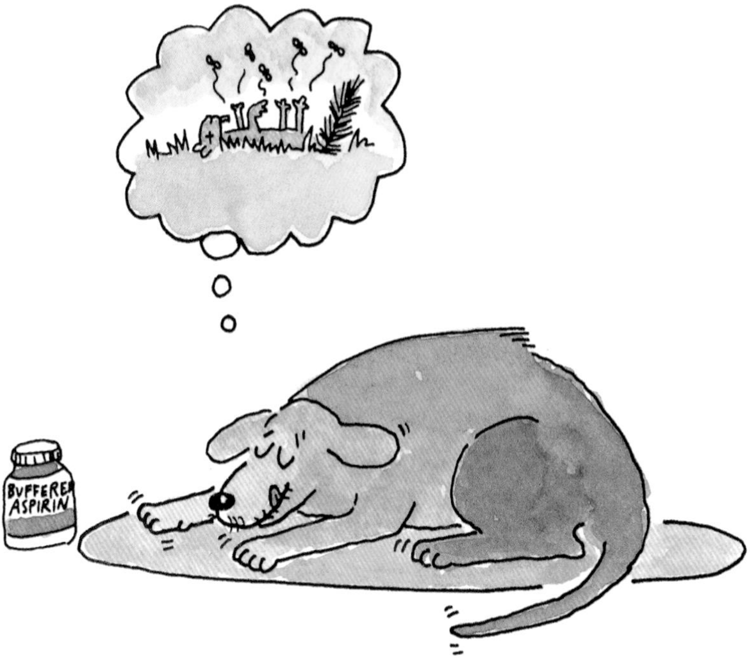
BUFFERED
ASPIRIN

AND THE ONLY DRUGS THEY TAKE ARE THE ONES YOU GIVE THEM

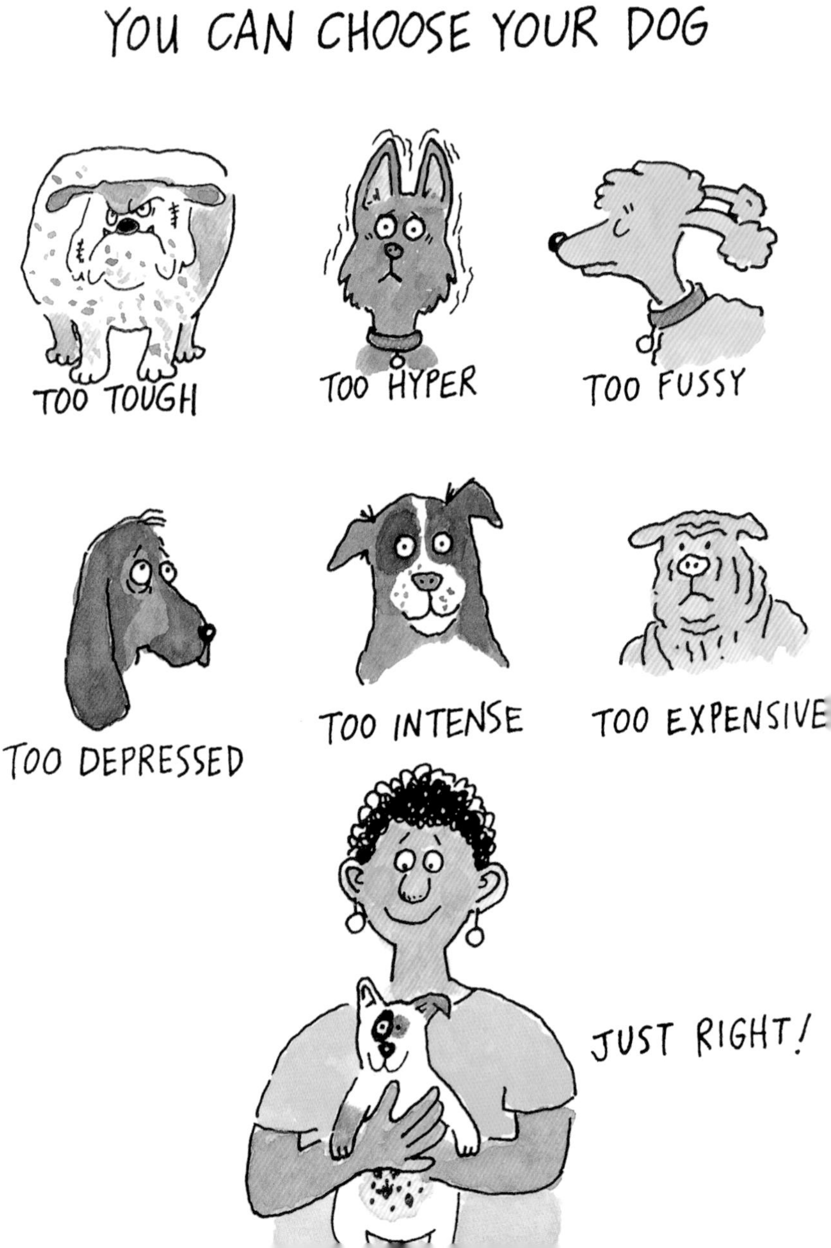
YOU CAN CHOOSE YOUR DOG
TOO TOUGH
TOO HYPER
TOO FUSSY
TOO DEPRESSED
TOO INTENSE
TOO EXPENSIVE
JUST RIGHT!

IF YOU WANT TO GO BACK TO SCHOOL AND YOU HAVE A DOG, IT'S NOT TOO DIFFICULT

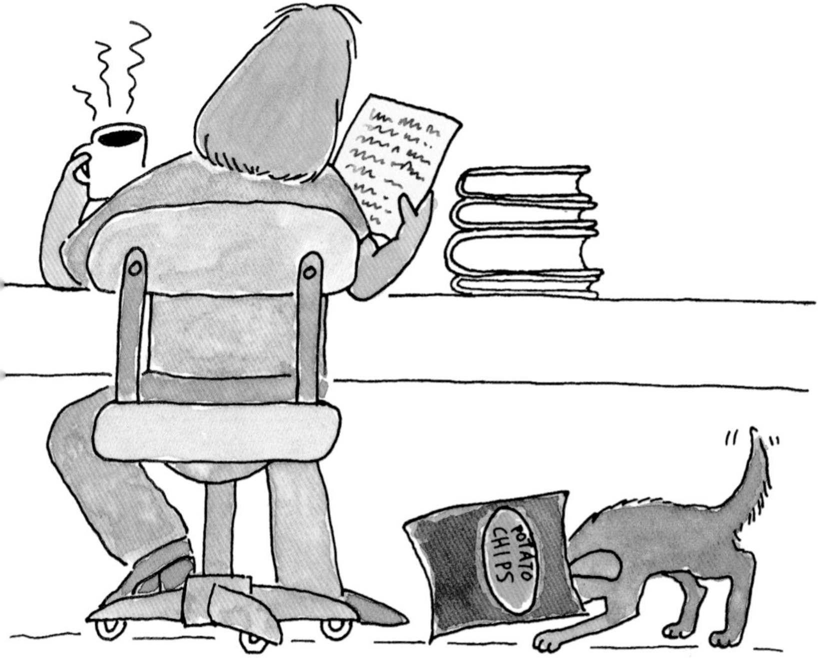
POTATO CHIPS

DOGS ARE NOT EMBARRASSED WHEN YOU SING IN PUBLIC

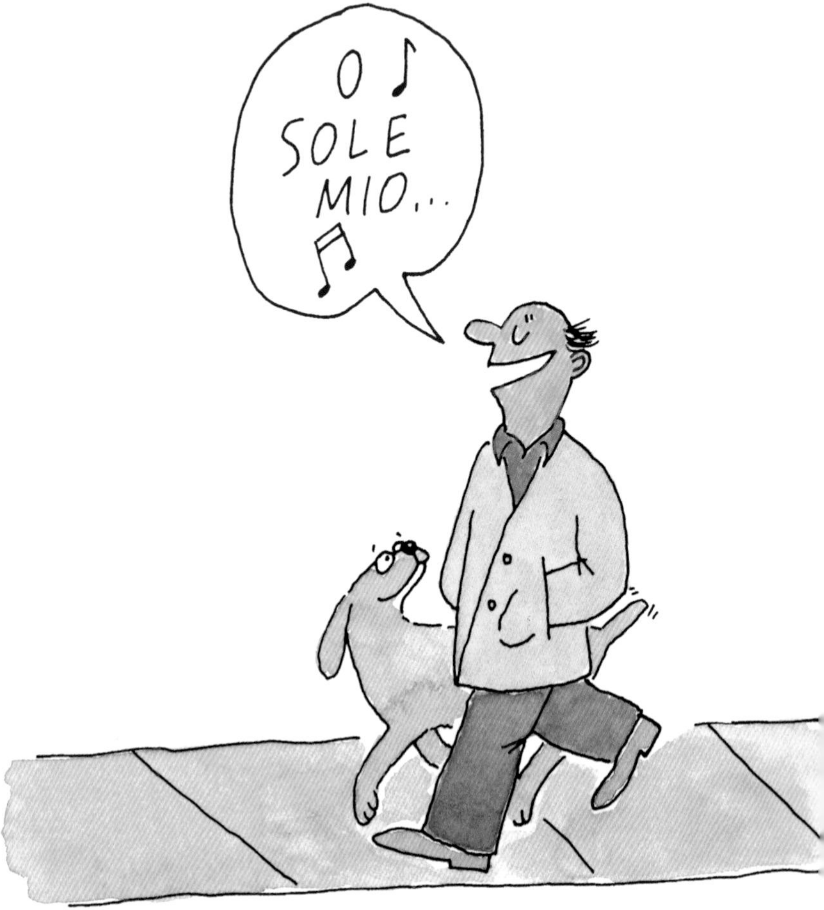
O SOLE MIO...

IF YOUR DOG IS DESTRUCTIVE, IT'S OKAY TO LEAVE IT IN A CAGE WHEN YOU HAVE TO GO OUT

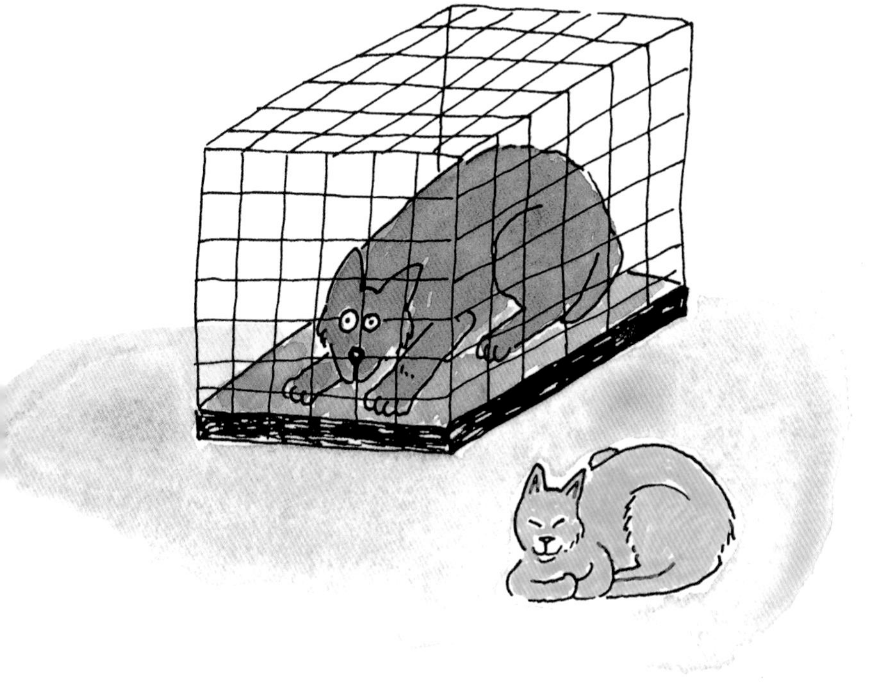

DOGS DON'T DEMAND BRAND-NAME SHOES

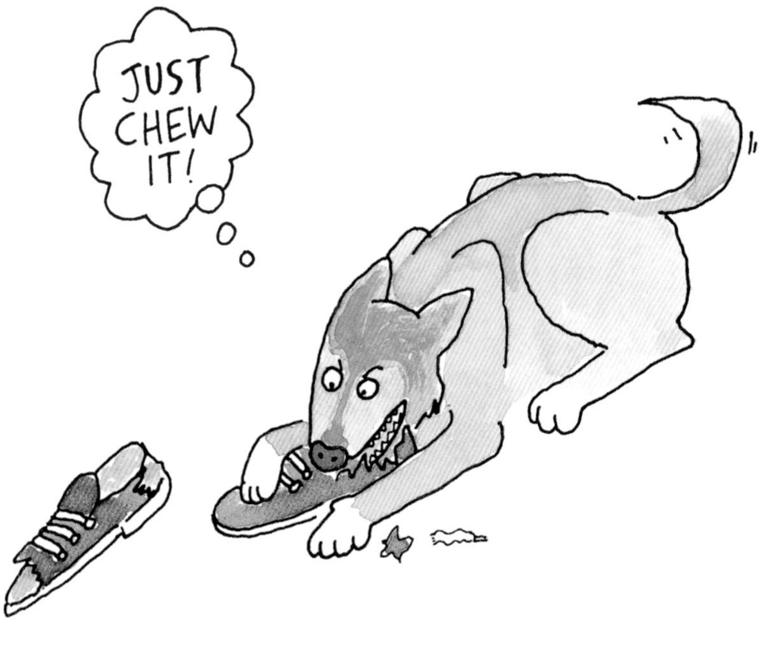
JUST CHEW IT!

YOU CAN CHOOSE ALL YOUR DOG'S FRIENDS

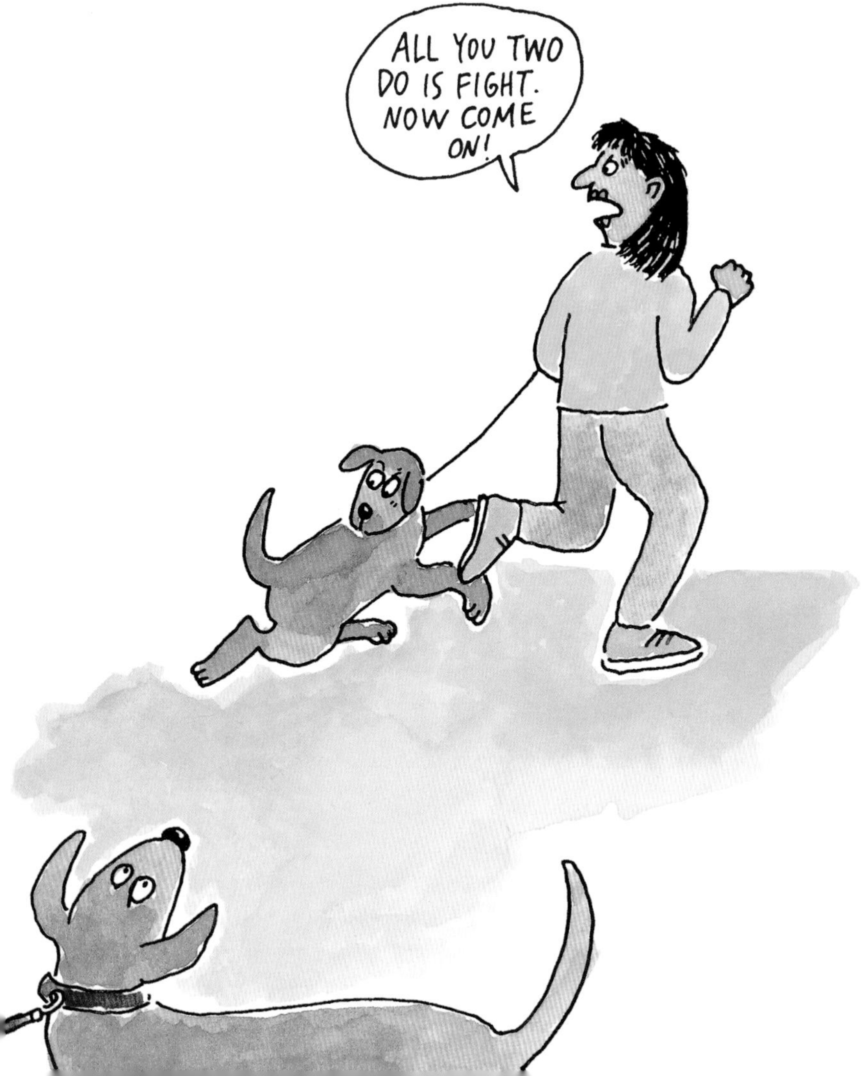
ALL YOU TWO DO IS FIGHT. NOW COME ON!

IF YOU HAVE YOUR FIRST DOG WHEN YOU
ARE SIXTEEN, NOBODY WILL JUDGE YOU

DOGS DON'T HOME IN ON YOUR FRIENDS' VULNERABILITIES RIGHT AWAY

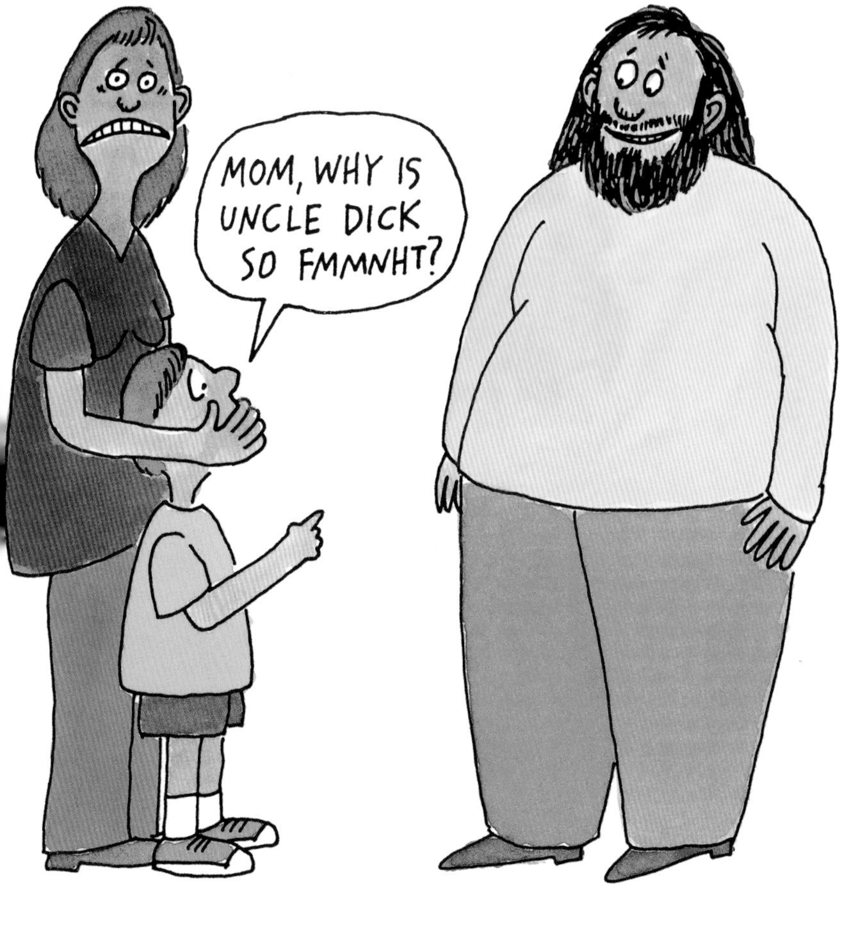
MOM, WHY IS UNCLE DICK SO FMMNHT?

DOGS THINK YOU ARE THE BEST PARENT IN THE WORLD. PERIOD.

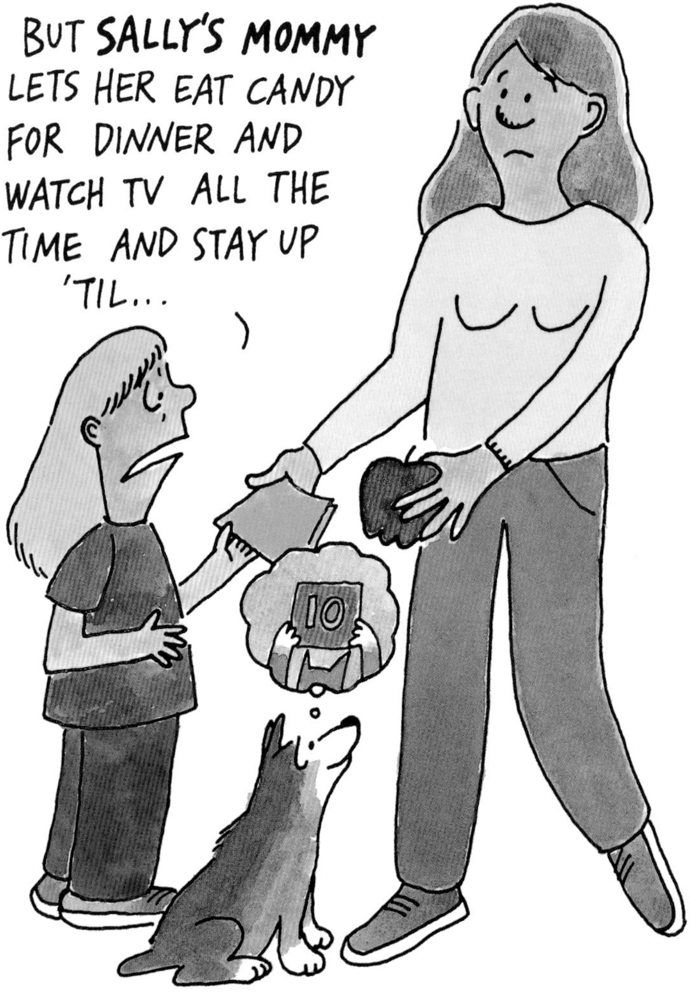
BUT **SALLY'S MOMMY** LETS HER EAT CANDY FOR DINNER AND WATCH TV ALL THE TIME AND STAY UP 'TIL...
10

THE CUTE PHASE OF A DOG LASTS ITS WHOLE LIFE

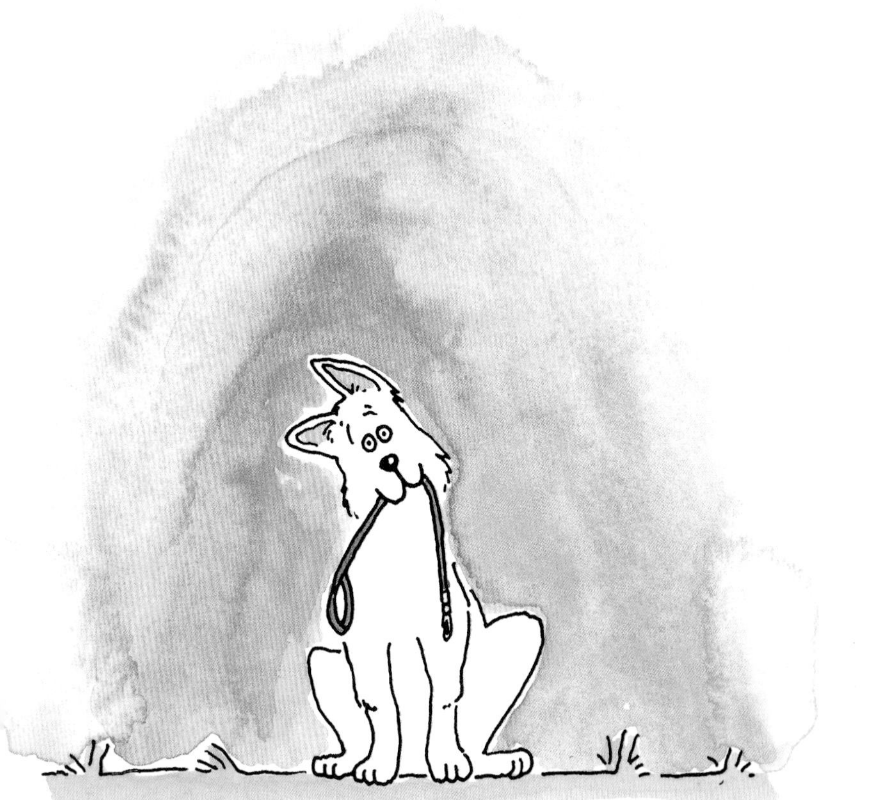

PART 2:

HOW KIDS AND DOGS ARE THE SAME

NEITHER PHONES HOME WHEN SHE'S LATE

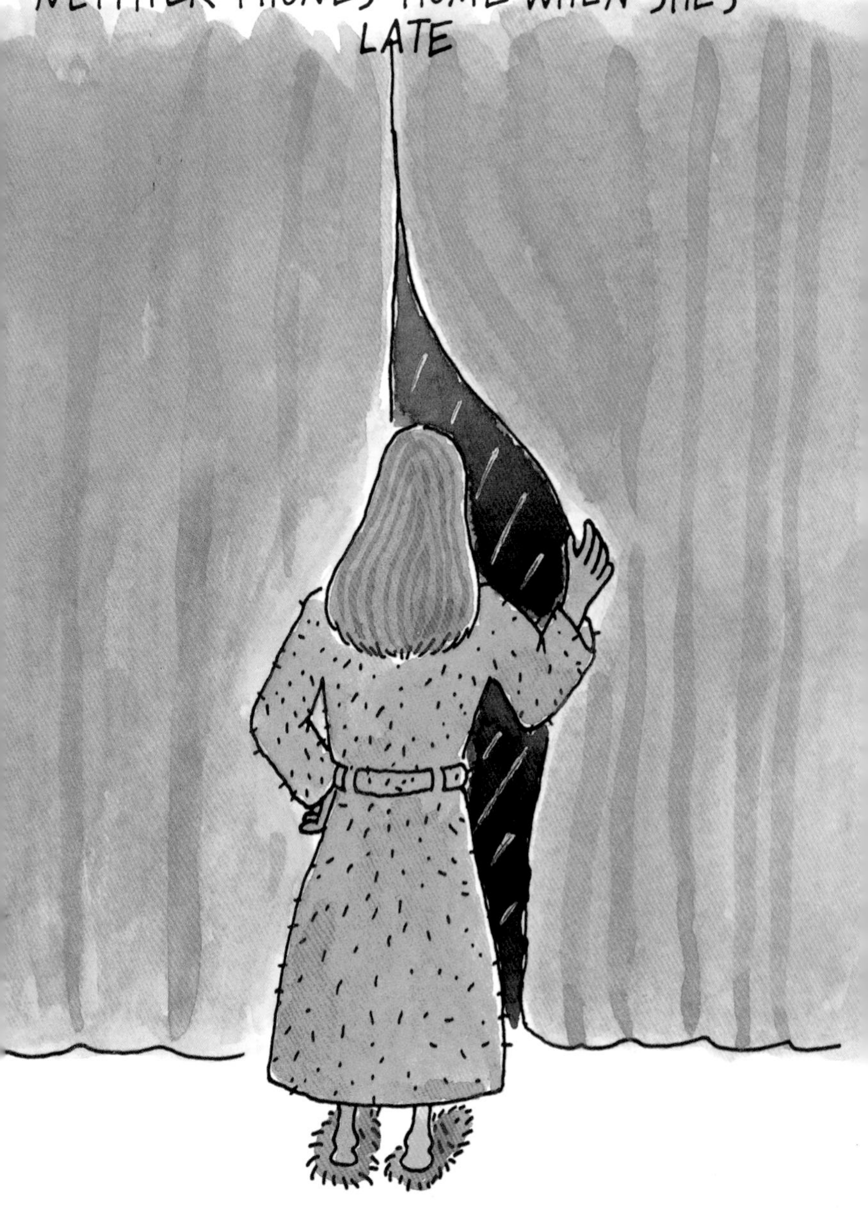

BOTH ARE COMPLETELY AWESTRUCK BY THE POTENTIAL OF AN OPEN REFRIGERATOR

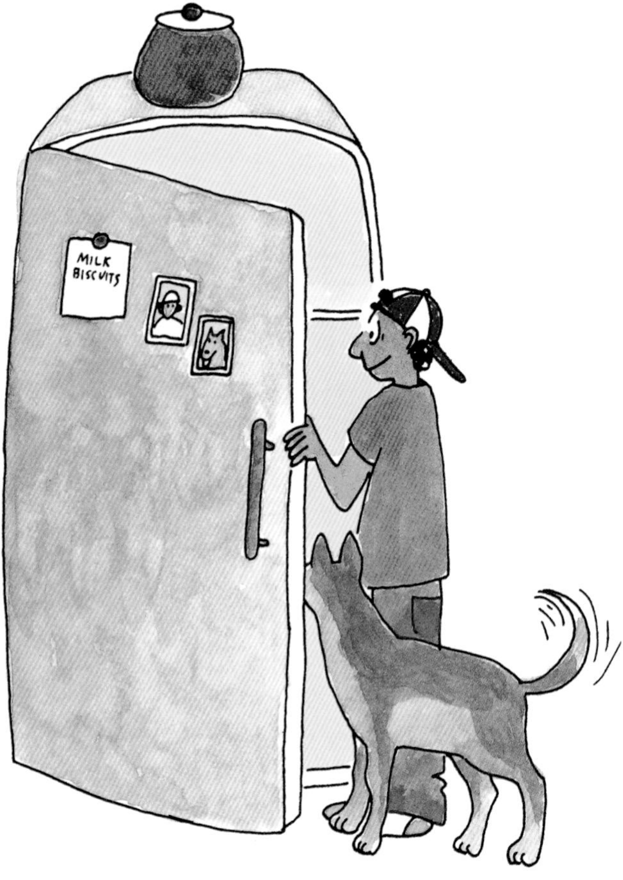
MILK
BISCUITS

BOTH FIND IT DIFFICULT TO SHARE TOYS

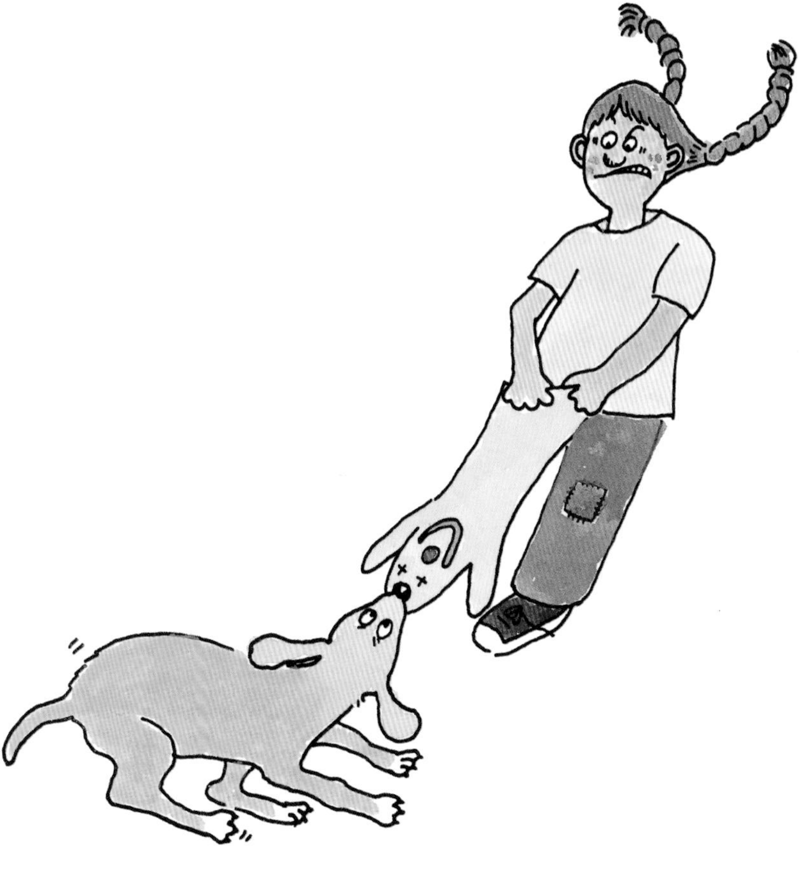

HAVING EITHER PRECLUDES THE IDEA OF A CLEAN LIVING ENVIRONMENT

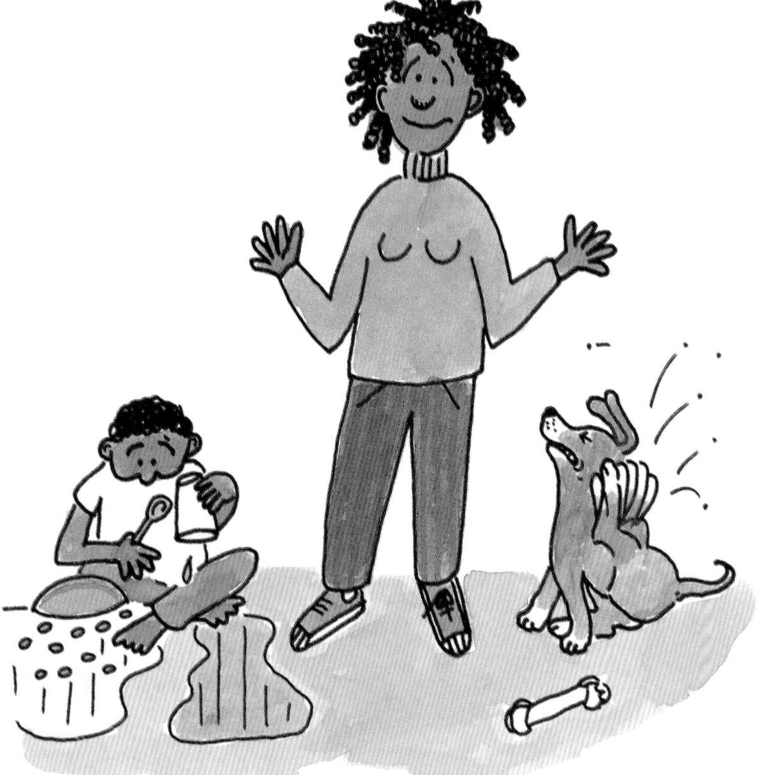

BOTH THINK FOOD THAT'S FALLEN ON THE GROUND TASTES BETTER (ESPECIALLY IF IT'S FROM AN ANONYMOUS DONOR)

BOTH LIKE HANGING OUT OF MOVING VEHICLES

YOU CAN KILL YOURSELF ON EITHER'S TOYS

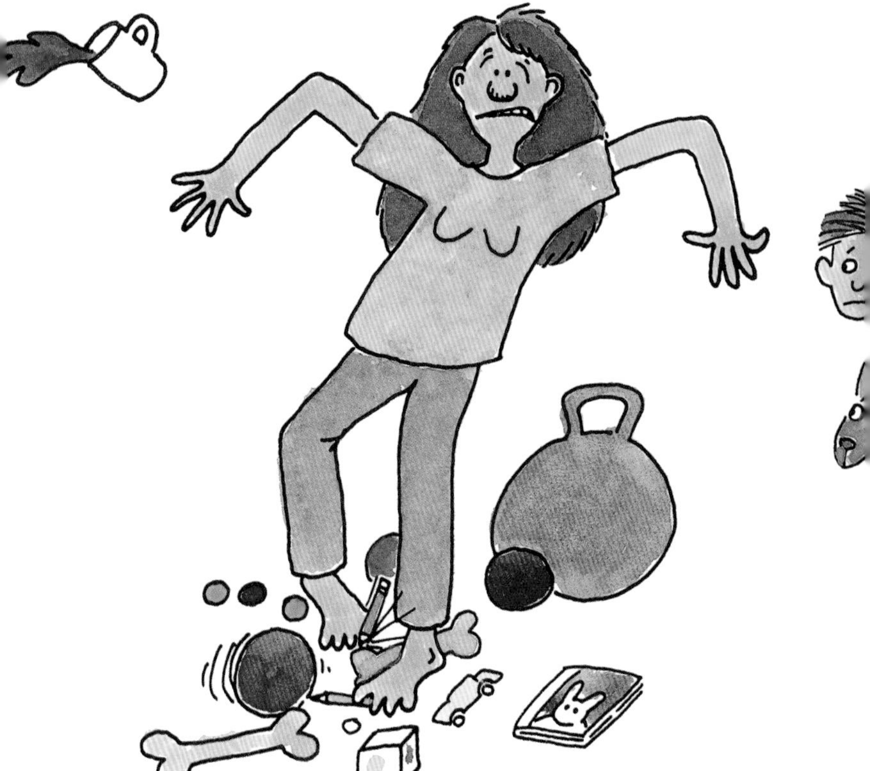

BOTH CONSIDER SAND A CULINARY FAVORITE

BOTH PREFER RUNNING AROUND NAKED

NEITHER RELAYS IMPORTANT PHONE MESSAGES

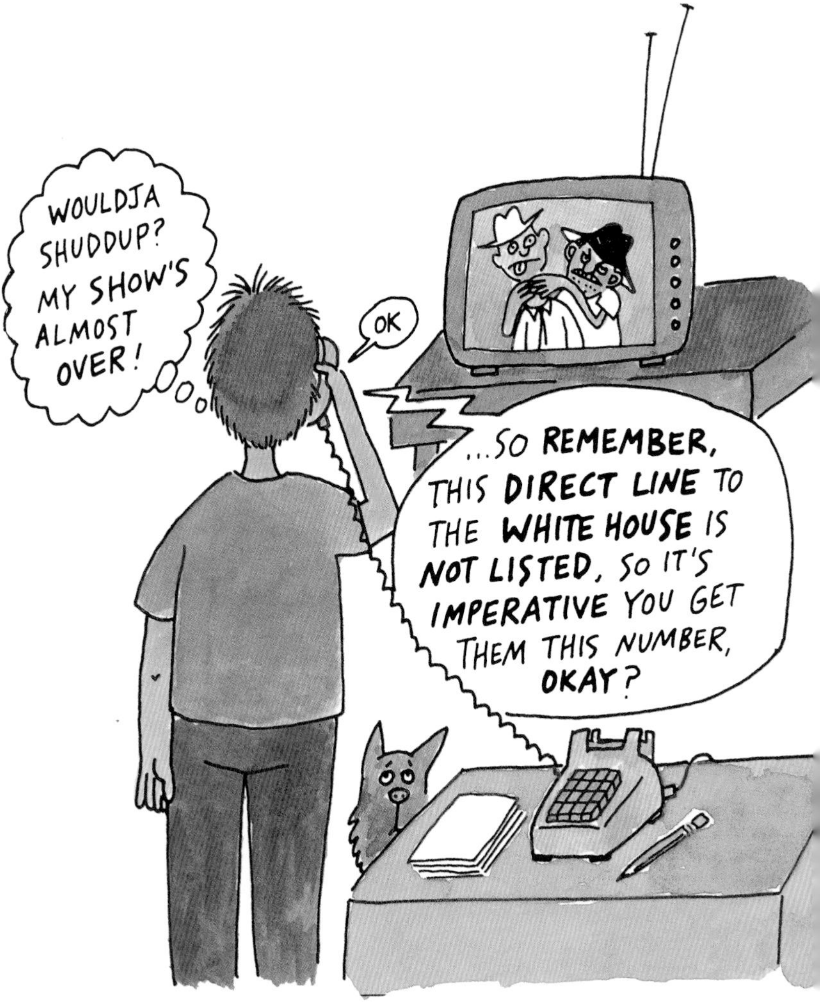
WOULDJA SHUDDUP? MY SHOW'S ALMOST OVER!
OK
...SO REMEMBER, THIS DIRECT LINE TO THE WHITE HOUSE IS NOT LISTED, SO IT'S IMPERATIVE YOU GET THEM THIS NUMBER, OKAY?

BOTH SUFFER FROM SELECTIVE DEAFNESS

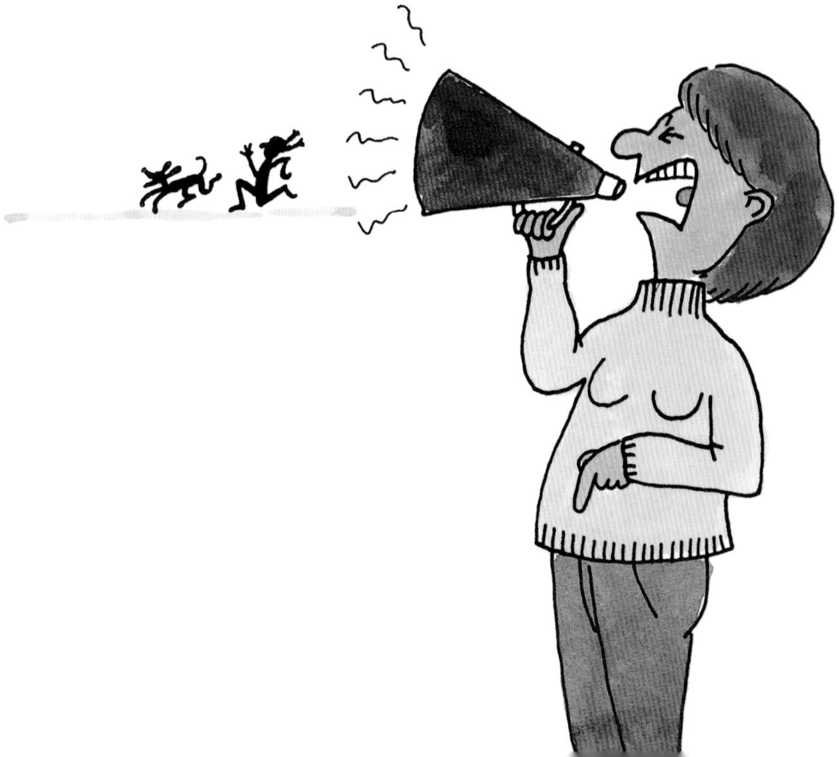

PEOPLE JUDGE YOU IF YOU SHARE
YOUR BED WITH EITHER

BOTH ARE HARD ON CATS

YOU WORRY THAT NEITHER WILL SURVIVE THEIR TEENS

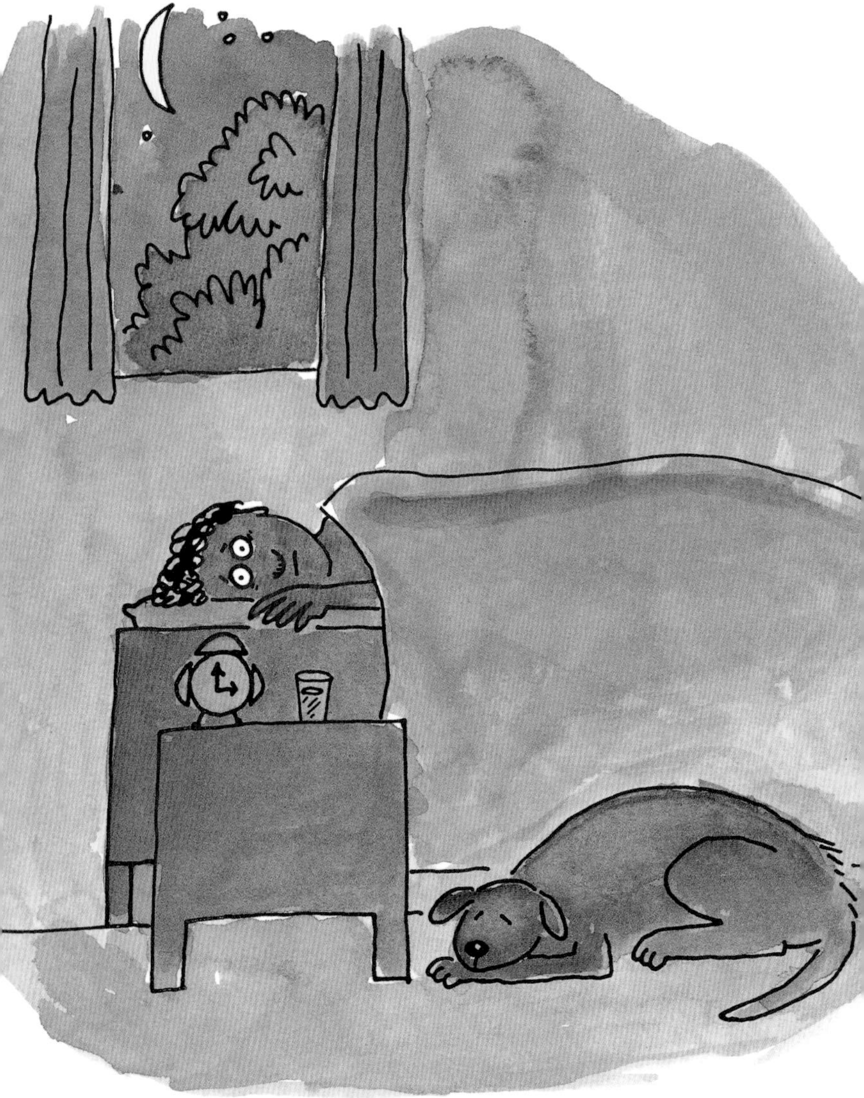

BOTH LIKE TO EAT TREATS ON THE FURNITURE

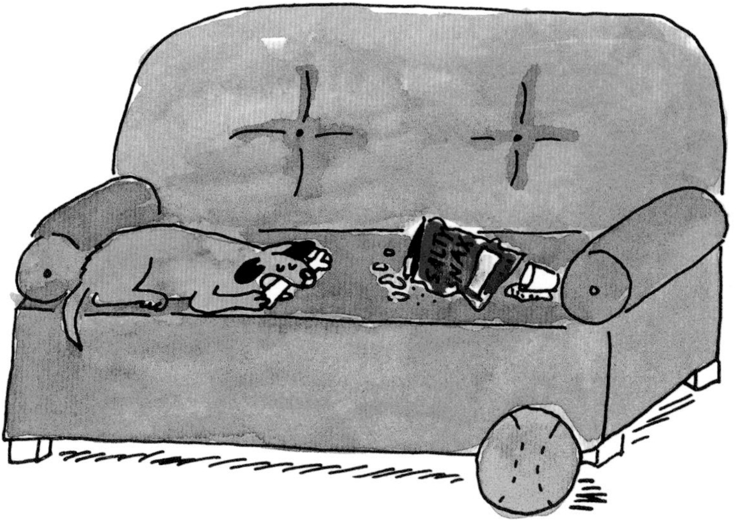
SALTY SNAX

BOTH HATE TO HAVE THEIR NAILS CLIPPED

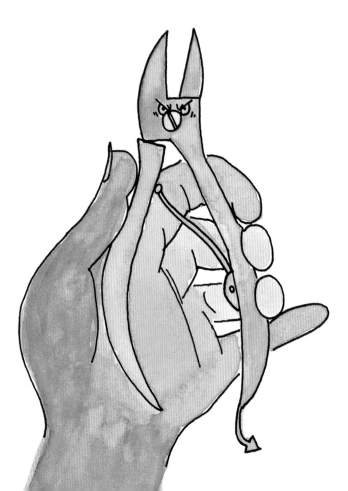

YOU CAN BORE FRIENDS & LOVED ONES SENSELESS WITH ENDLESS STORIES OF EITHER

NEITHER WILL BE THERE TO TAKE CARE OF YOU WHEN YOU GET OLD...

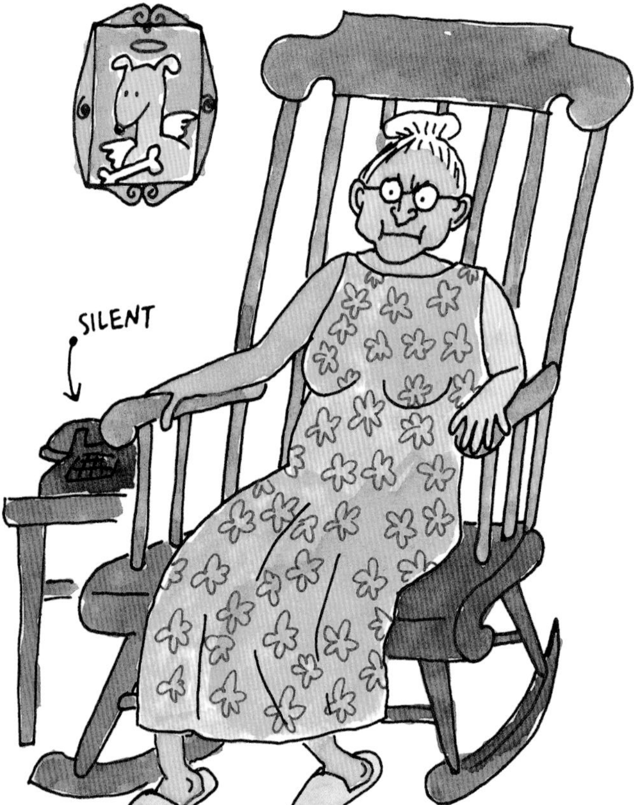
SILENT

PART 3:

WHY KIDS ARE BETTER THAN DOGS

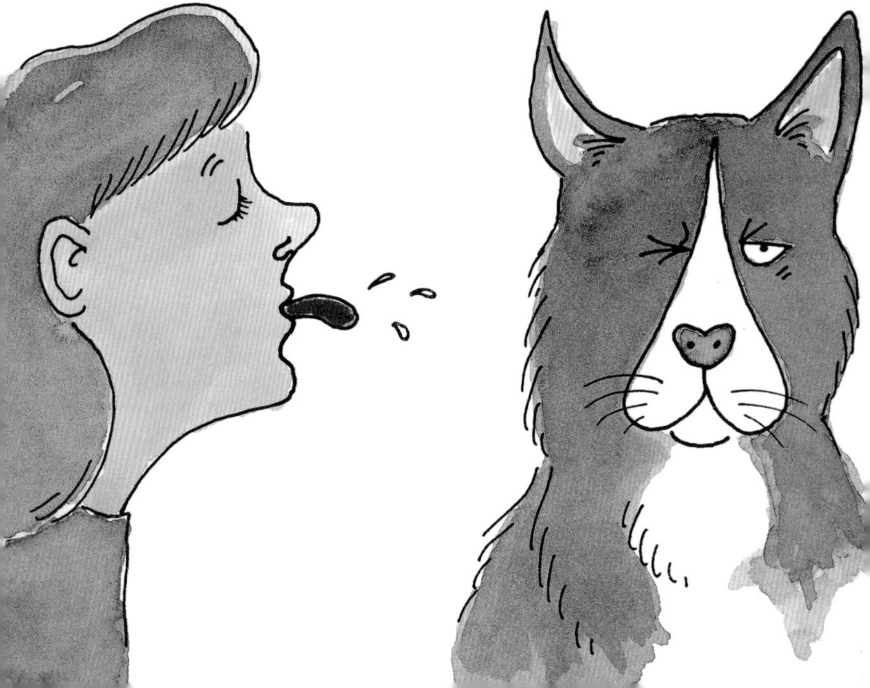

NOBODY THROWS PUPPY SHOWERS

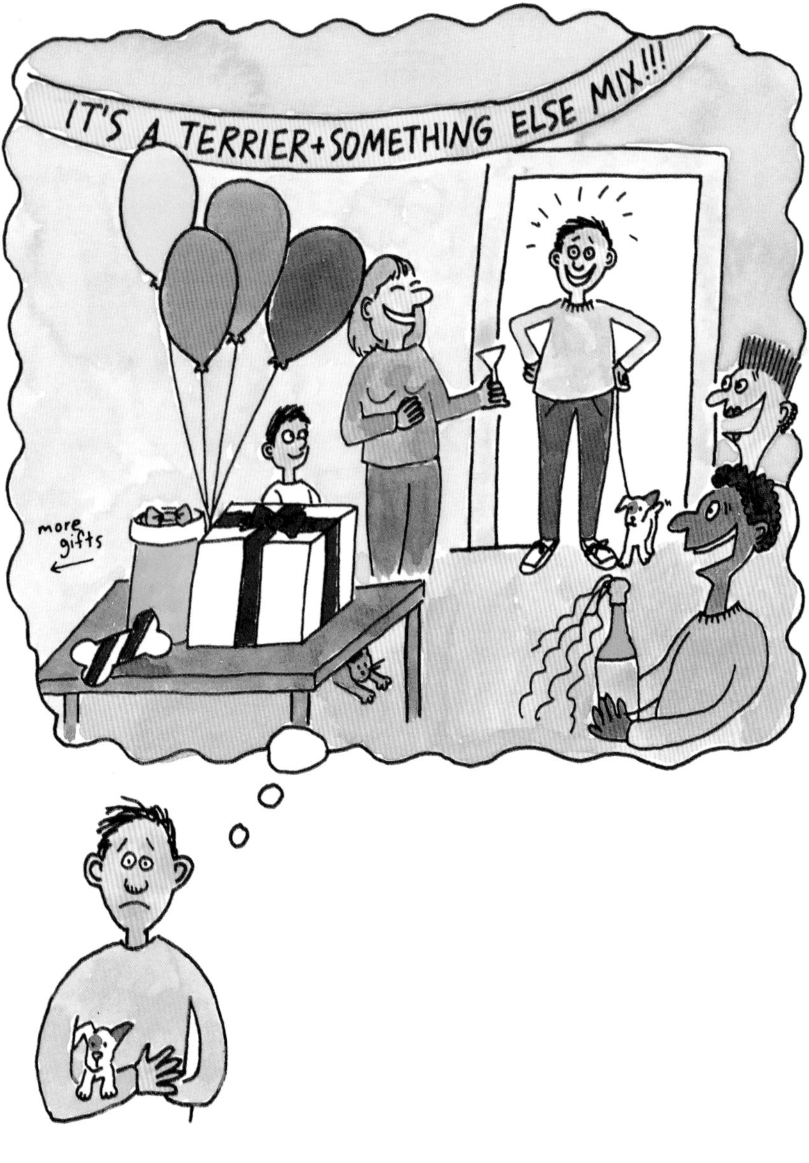
IT'S A TERRIER+SOMETHING ELSE MIX!!!
more gifts

KIDS WON'T GIVE YOU ASTHMA

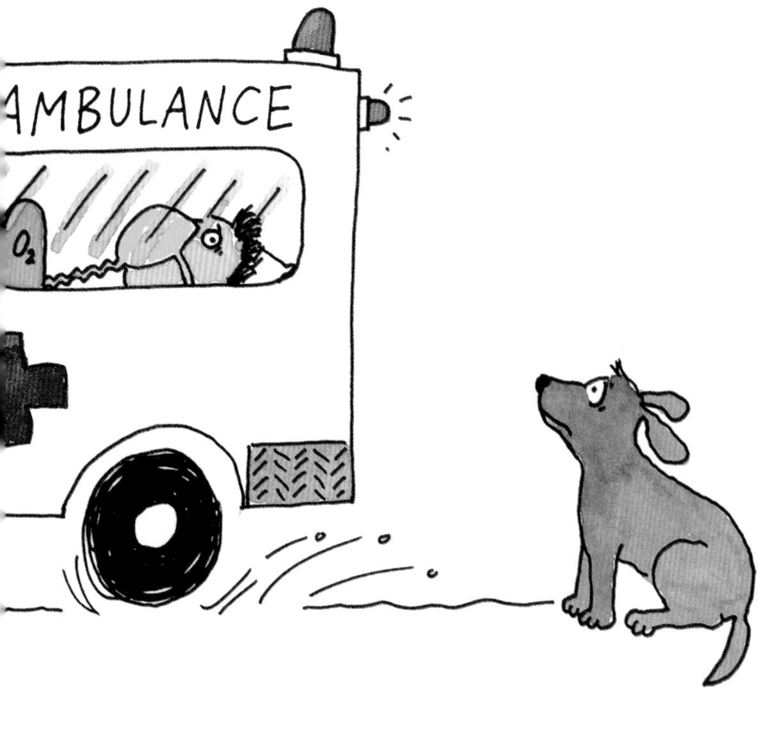
AMBULANCE
O_2

KIDS DON'T CONSIDER CAT TURDS A
DELICACY

KIDS DON'T DRINK OUT OF THE TOILET

KIDS DON'T EAT POOP

KIDS CAN TELL YOU WHEN THEY'RE ABOUT TO THROW UP IN THE CAR

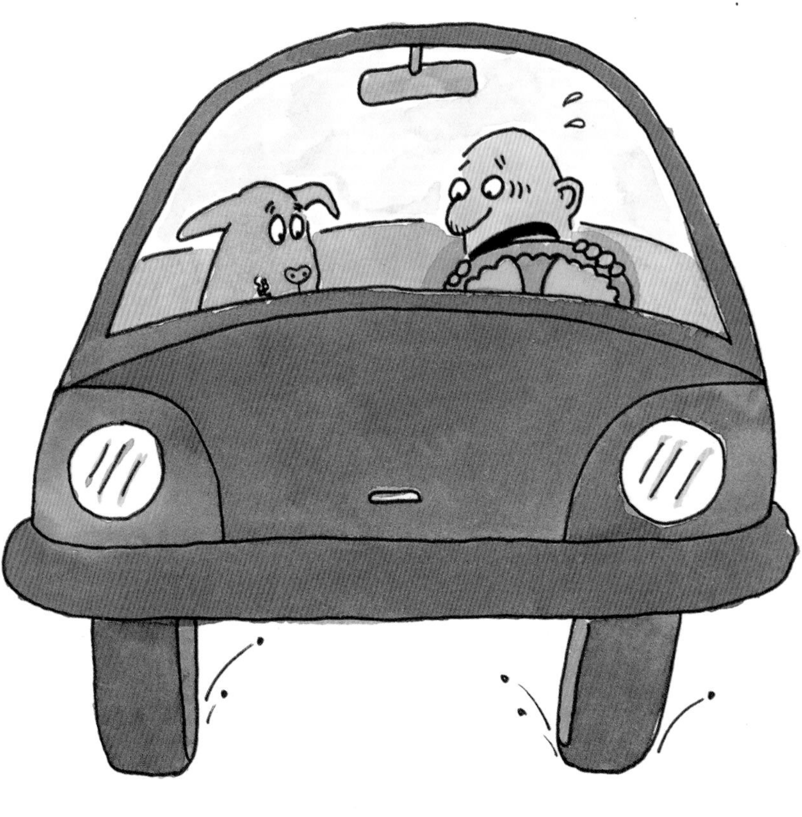

IT'S MORE ACCEPTABLE TO CARRY A PICTURE OF YOUR KID IN YOUR WALLET

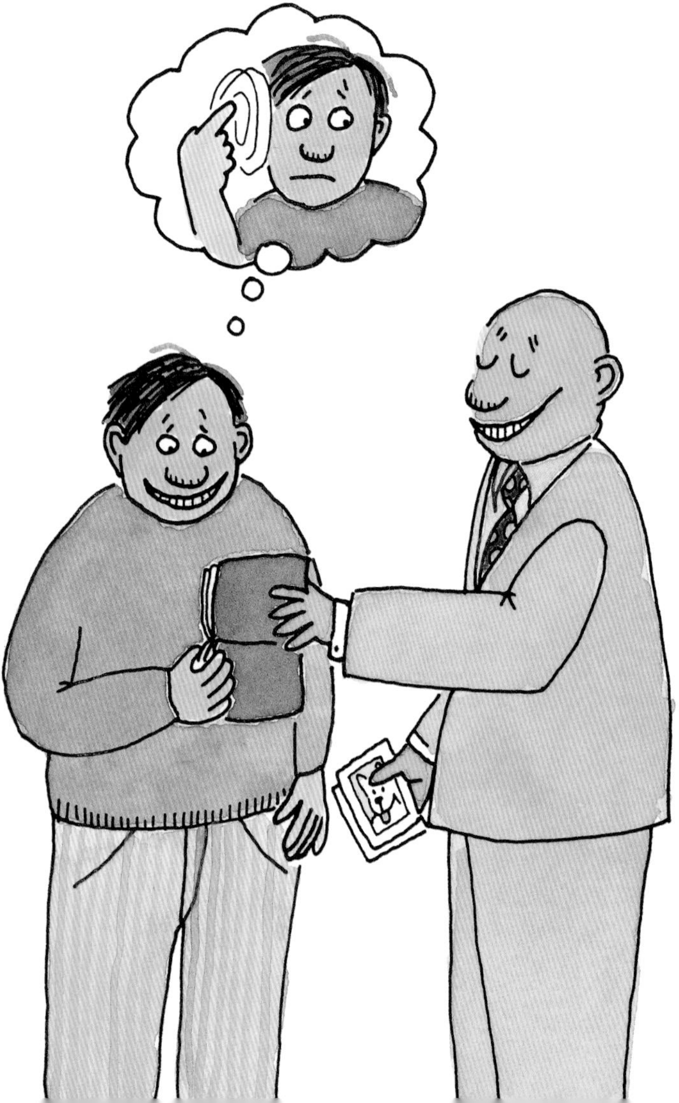

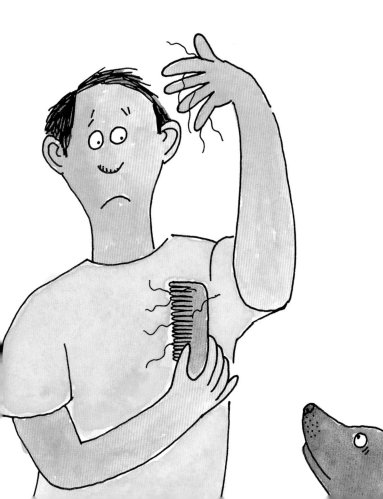

KIDS DON'T START TO SHED UNTIL THEY'VE LEFT HOME

KIDS WON'T SCARF DOWN DEAD FISH ON THE BEACH

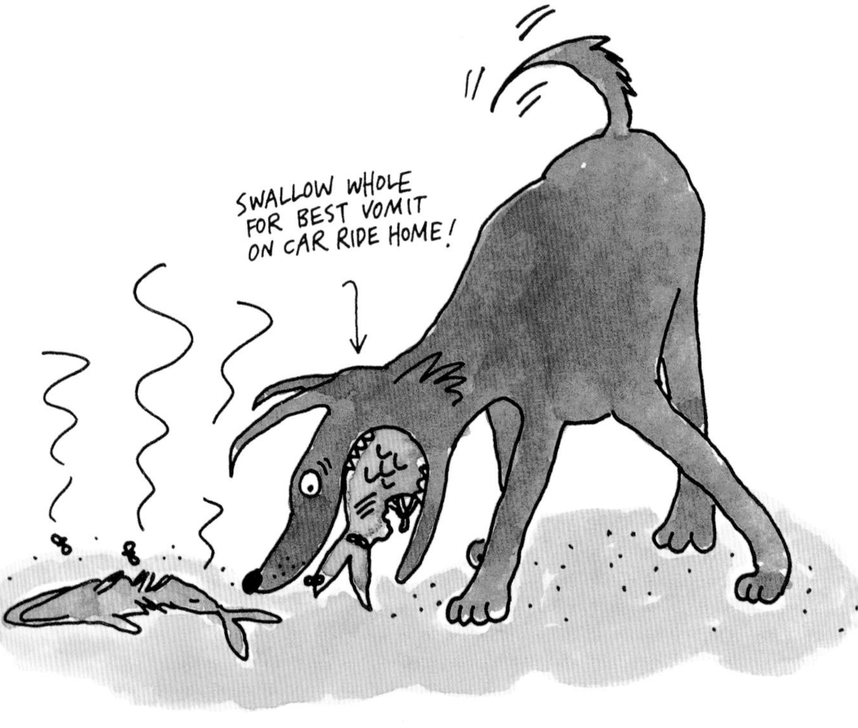
SWALLOW WHOLE FOR BEST VOMIT ON CAR RIDE HOME!

(THE BAD NEWS IS THEY WON'T EAT THE DEAD FISH YOU SPENT $15.99/LB ON, EITHER!)

KIDS WON'T HUMP YOUR BOSS'S LEG

"FAMILY LEAVE TIME" IS NOT OFFERED FOR NEW PUPPIES

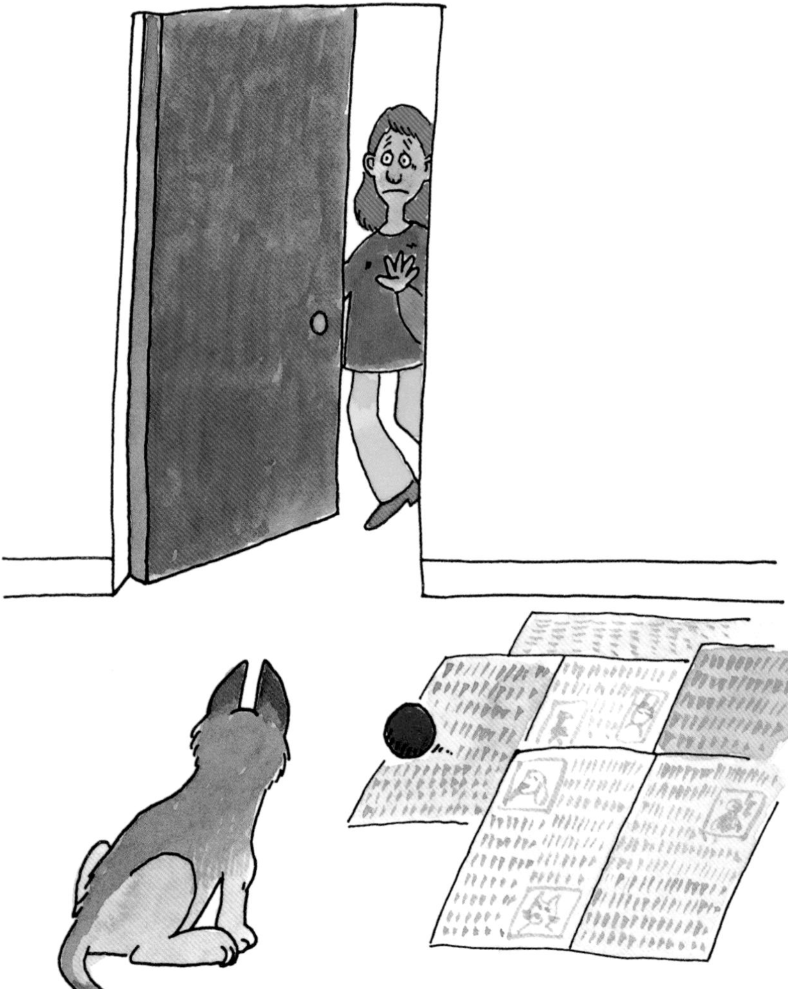

KIDS CAN TEACH YOU HOW TO WORK YOUR COMPUTER

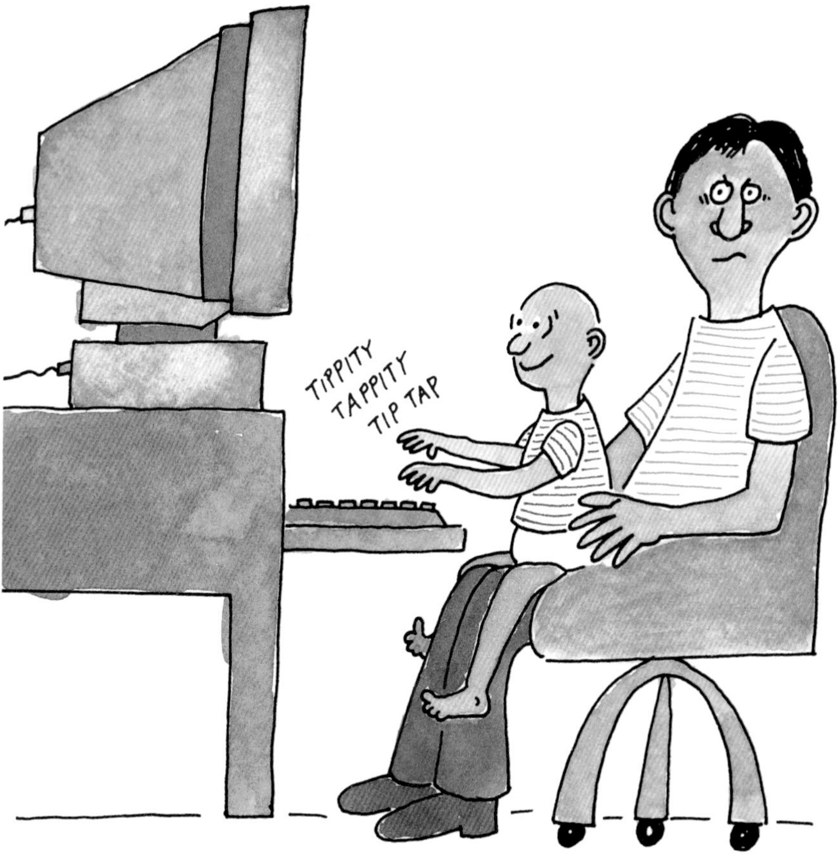
TIPPITY
TAPPITY
TIP TAP

KIDS DON'T EAT DIRTY UNDERWEAR AND SOCKS

KIDS DON'T ROLL ON DEAD THINGS

IT'S EASIER TO BATHE A KID

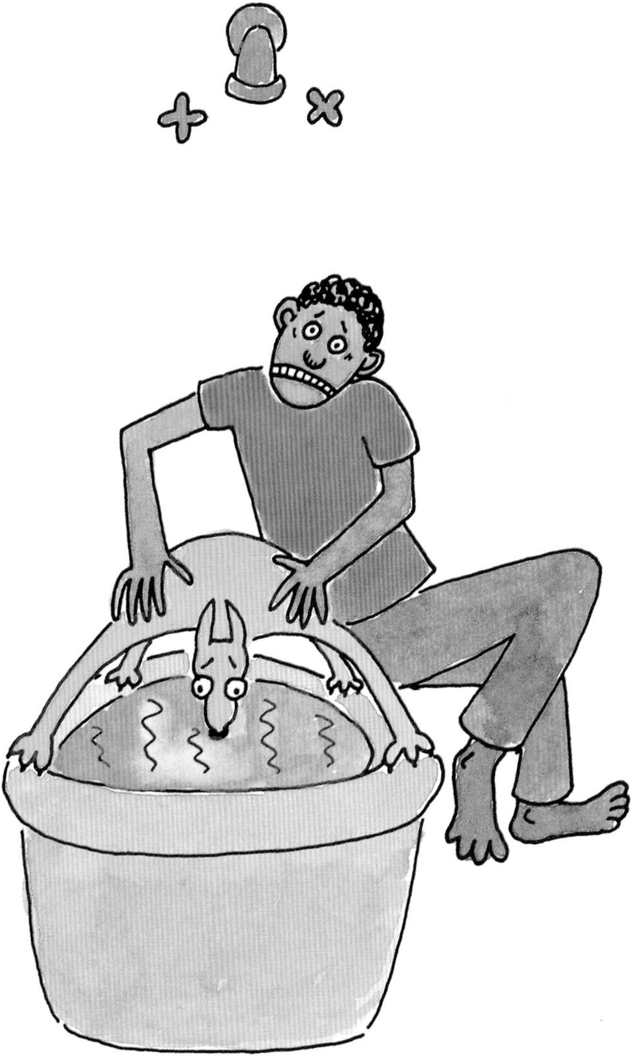

KIDS CAN TELL YOU WHERE IT HURTS

KIDS ARE DESIGNED TO LAST LONGER THAN DOGS

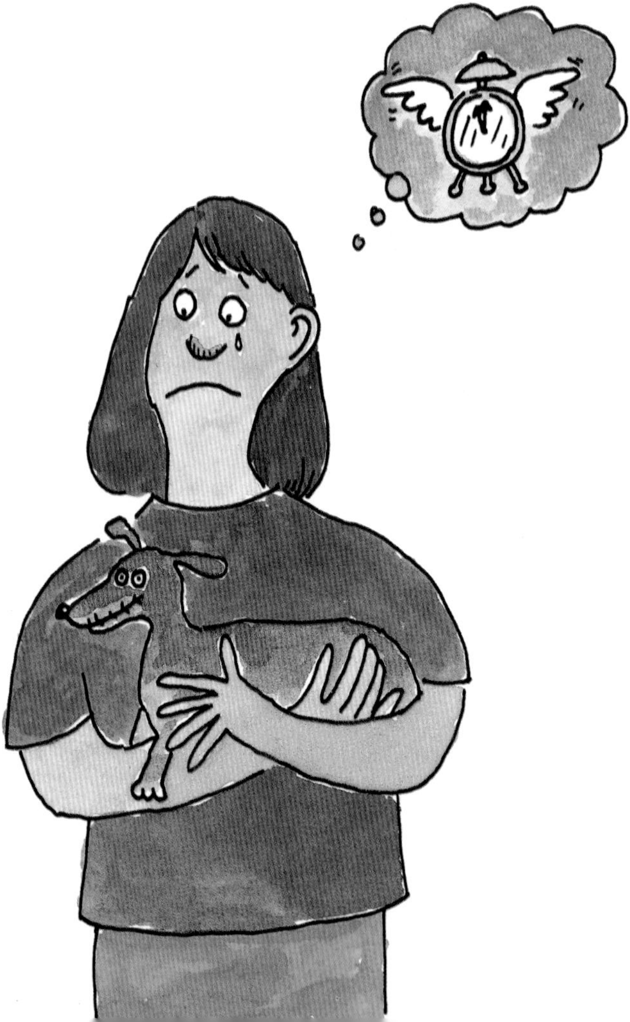